*This book is dedicated to a...
and girls who welcomed me...
adopted home of Walworth .... London and
all my fellow Glaswegians living there.*

Thanks for the memories.

Lifetime and Adventures
of a
Gorbals Bricklayer
in South London

[Elephant/Walworth, etc]

Danny Gill

ISBN: 9798562581068

PublishNation
www.publishnation.co.uk

Other books by Danny Gill which can be bought on Lulu.com and Amazon, either as a paperback or a Kindle e-book.

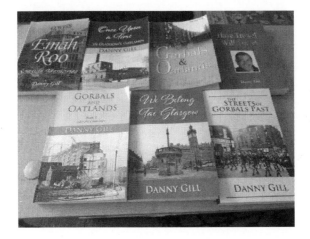

All proceeds from this book go to:

The upkeep of the Southern Necropolis Graveyard on Caledonia Road in the Gorbals area of Glasgow close to where I grew up; and

The Benny Lynch statue campaign. (Benny was Scotland's first ever boxing world champion.)

My sincerest thanks to everyone who purchases this book.

Danny Gill
2020

Contents

Preface

In my book I tell of all my adventures while living and working in the South London area of the Metropolis, the main thrust of my book will be about the Elephant /Walworth area of South London although I also lived/ worked in other parts including Camberwell, Peckham, Bermondsey, Brixton, New Cross, Kennington and Lambeth.

I worked on the construction of the large Heygate, Aylesbury and Salisbury estates and other buildings too in the Elephant/Walworth area which many of you reading my book may have lived on.

Altogether I lived in the Elephant/Walworth area for 26 years, six years overseas in different counties and 20 years working and living in between South, North, West and East London although out of that 20 years only eighteen months was spent living outside of South London.

I have many good memories of working on the various sites and will hopefully trigger your memory of some of the Pubs that I mention, the streets where I lived on, the cafes and shops etc I used.

When I arrived in London aged 20 in 1968 I have to say that London was going through the same upheaval that my native city of Glasgow was going through with the demolition of the old dwellings and the construction of new housing estates, it seemed everywhere you looked there were tower cranes and places known to people for years were fast disappearing.

In fact if you look at a photo of the Elephant in say the mid 1950's and compared it with today then you would think you had landed on another planet but as they say that's progress for you. Although lots of people will hanker to be back in the "old days" and there's no shame in that at all.

I was a young man of 20 as I said when I landed in London and there was no one to meet me coming off the train at Euston railway station and had to find my own digs and work but work for the building trade was no problem.

The only problem I had was I didn't know the names of different areas in London or what buses to get so I had to learn the hard way.

I remember looking at the London tube map and it looked as if someone had squeezed twelve different coloured toothpastes all over it Lol but with the passing of time and many a mistake made I slowly but surely would find my way about.

What made me come to London ?, well when I was serving my five year apprenticeship in Glasgow all the seasoned travelled bricklayers told me to "go to London son it's the home of bricklayers" and this I found out to be very true.

I spent the first seven months of living in London over at the Kings cross area, so how did I come to live and work round the Elephant/Walworth area well it all starts in chapter 1 of my book.

Are you ready to join me in my "lifetime and adventures of a Gorbals bricklayer living in South London"?

I think you will enjoy my roller coaster life, in general life was good to me but sometimes I would meet set-backs and when that happened I just dusted myself down and said to myself right Danny boy upwards and onwards.

From the first chapter to the last chapter in my books Part 1 it's all about living in South London but in my books Part 2 I will go through my life and adventures overseas and any area outside of South London that I lived/worked in, because its all intertwined of leaving and coming back to South London.

In some of my books chapters I have changed the name of the person[s] I am talking about , this is to stop any embarrassment to them or family members I will state "lets call them" or "lets call him/her", as I have no wish to offend anyone, but the story's must go in as its all part of my lifetime and adventures.

I may get the year mixed up as its hard to be spot on thinking back to all those years but I wouldn't be that far out and it doesn't really affect the story line.

- - - - -

Acknowledgements

I would first of all like to thank all the the Cockney boys and girls who welcomed me with open arms when I made South London my adopted home.

For my photos and info in the book I would like to thank, Les Allen, Peter Bonnen, John Cooper, Michael James Dunham, Wendy Egan, Susan D. Fitzgerald, Ray Denis Johnson, Darren Lock, Lambeth archives, London Metropolitan archives, Richard Lyons, Robert Lyons, Tony Robbins, Southwark news, South London press, Sue Wilson, Wikapedia. [plus lots of my own photos.]

Also a big thanks to everyone of you who takes the time to read my lifetime and adventures.

Last but not least, many thanks to David and Gwen at PublishNation for giving me another book to be proud of.

Part 1

Chapter 1

Arriving to Work in South London

My first sight of South London was in 1968 aged 20 when I went to work on the construction of Perronet house at London rd opposite the Bakerloo tube line. There was an advert in Friday nights Evening news newspaper for bricklayers wanted to help build Perronet house. I phoned up the given number, it was a bricklaying agency called Adams and Hawkins and they were paying £5 - 10/- per shift and I was to contact Pat the foreman bricklayer on Monday morning for an eight o'clock start.

[Photo of Perronet house at the Elephant which was later refurbished.]

I turned up at Perronet house Monday morning and so did another bricklayer called Mick form New Cross, Pat the foreman said "right I'll put the two of you working together", we were told to go up to the sixth floor and we would be building face brickwork along the corridors that separated the flats from the corridor.

Anyway Mick was a good bricklayer too and a nice lad to work with, when we had a minutes break waiting on our hod carrier bringing us mortar and Mick pointed over the skyline and said "that's the new Elephant indoor shopping area just built a few years ago and behind it is the area of South London called Walworth".

[Photo of the then newly opened indoor shopping centre at the Elephant.]

"They say they are going to build a new housing estate there which will be called the Heygate estate" and me never thinking for a moment that not only would I be on the building of the Heygate but later I would be married and live with my wife Mo [Maureen] and our three children on this estate. Working on the construction of Perronet house was the first time that I had set eyes on South London and I liked working there with Mick. We had three breaks a day, breakfast, lunch and afternoon tea break [15 minute] we started at eight am and finished at five o'clock.

Quite a few of the bricklayers and other trades went for a couple of pints and a ham/cheese roll at Lunch time to the Princess of Wales which was at the corner of Princess st/London rd right beside Perronet house, this was the accepted daily occurrence but I only went to the pub at lunch time on a Friday for a pint as this was us almost at the start of the weekend and made me feel good. Some of the guys who had a few pints at lunch time would also go back into the pub at three o'clock for another pint [at tea break]. Remember it was three o'clock closing time for the pubs back then but the landlord allowed the workers a few minutes grace, of course that wouldn't happen today with all the health and safety rules and back in those days you could smoke openly on site again not like today. !!

Come Fridays and Pat the foreman would pay us out at five o'clock and it was all cash in your wage packets those days, no bank accounts for us bricklayers back in those days. Anyway Mick said to me "Danny look at how many wage packets Pat has still left", we were the last two to get paid, Pat had a few wage packets still in his jacket pocket. Mick said to me have you ever heard of "dead men" and I said it was what we called empty bottles of beer in Glasgow.

Mick laughed and said "no what happens is the foreman and the site agent make a deal, as its all on a day work basis, who's to know how many men are on site so Pat could tell his Governor that there were ten bricklayers and five hod carriers on site but there might only be eight bricklayers and four hoddies. So that was an extra three wage packets to be split between the foreman and the site agent as it was the site agent who signed a daily or weekly time sheet stating how many men were on site". Of course Pat might not have been on the "fiddle" but there were plenty who were back in those days of cash payments.

I had been on the building of Perronet house for about five months, so that was a total of eight months that I had been living in London at the Kings cross area and I'll be truthful I became a wee bit home sick. I hadn't seen my Ma or Da or mates in that time and also missed watching my football team Glasgow Celtic play on Saturdays, so I finished up work and caught the train back to Glasgow. It was good to be back home again and see my Parents and sister, I had started work more or less straight away on landing in Glasgow and was working beside this other bricklayer called Bobby Morrison who said to me one day, "have you ever worked down in the "Big smoke" before" and I said yes I had worked in London for eight months. Bobby said do you fancy coming down to London with me to work and I answered yes, he said "that's good, I have a mate called Richie Humphries who lives in Walworth and lives in a place called Blendon row".

We got the train down to London but that night before the train left we had a farewell drink with our girlfriends, I had met this girl called Jean at the dance hall and things were looking good. She didn't want me to go but I wanted so much to go to this place called Walworth. Bobby's girlfriend Theresa didn't want him to go either but go we did with the promise of writing letters, remember no mobile phones back in those days !!.

We landed in London and got digs out at Grays Inn rd and started work with a brickwork sub contractor called George Batt [who turned out to be a ["wrong un"] building an office block at Holborn. Come the first Saturday we weren't working Bobby said to me "right let me take you over to Walworth and meet my pal Richie", we caught the 45 bus and got off at East st market or the Lane as it's commonly called. When we turned into the Lane I couldn't believe my eyes there were barrows/stalls that seemed to be stretched a mile long and the stall owners all shouting out their wares to attract the customers, it was packed with people and such a buzz and to be truthful I fell in love with the place straight away.

Bobby said right lets get to the pub which was the Good Intent and it was packed but his mate Richie was sitting in the back of the pub with a few Scots and Cockney lads. After the introductions and having a good drink Richie was regaling us with story's and jokes and we were all rolled up laughing, I though this is the life and by the way Andy Storrie was one of the Scots lads there that day, Andy was from Glasgow too and we became very good friends over the years.

After that day I would make frequent visits over to the Lane and have a drink with Richie and Andy in the Good Intent, the Bell and the Masons pubs which were all on the Lane, I loved going over there and thought to myself one day I will live here. Back to working with this George Batt, he paid Bobby and me £6 per shift which was good money. This George started to pay us a bit short on the third Friday saying he had bank trouble, we smelled a rat and told him on a Friday morning "we want all the money you owe us tonight as we are finished working with you". Come Friday afternoon he had all our money for us, so it was goodbye to him. On the Saturday morning we had no work and had a good drink in the pubs over Kings cross and at closing time Bobby said to me "I'm going to the Tattoo parlour to get Theresa's name tattooed on my arm and I said yes and I will get Jean's name tattooed on my arm" [a big mistake which I will tell you about later in my book].

Anyway there was an advert for bricklayers up in Manchester in the Evening News newspaper so we caught the train up to Manchester but I wont mention that story here I will mention it in Part 2 of my book as I want the main part of my book to be about South London.

While working in Manchester, Bobby and me had a falling out, I mean we were living in the same room, working together and drinking together it just got too much so we parted company and I headed back down to London.

I went to Camberwell green which had a few newsagents shop windows advertising rooms to let and got a room at Coldharbour lane that was the end nearest to Denmark hill and only seven bus stops from East street. I was working on this big new housing estate almost opposite my digs for bricklaying sub contractors called Peter Smith and Charlie Gates, I never liked this Peter Smith I think he came from Crystal Palace but Charlie was OK he came from Beckingham.

*[Photo of my digs in Coldharbour lane,
right hand door and top room.]*

There were six other bricklayers there and I got on very good with them all. It was a real big housing estate and this Peter and Charlie had two block of flats to build while there was another gang of bricklayers there who worked directly for the main contractor who was JJ Dean. They had three blocks of flats to build and there was actually a pub called the Robin Hood built on this estate by them.

[There was a girl who worked in the site canteen who always tried to flirt with me, lets call her "Betty" and to my eternal shame she comes into my story later.]

When I finished work at night I was having a drink in the pubs at Camberwell but after a few weeks would get the bus down to Walworth rd and drink in the pubs there and I was meeting up at night times with people I had met while having a drink with Richie and Andy Storrie which was great.

Some nights I would drink in the "Rock" ran by Charlie and his wife Sylvie [and their son young Charlie] or the Red Lion opposite the Rock or the Bell in the Lane or sometimes the Masons just past Portland st. I was getting to know lots of mates down Walworth rd and the Lane and as I said I liked the friendliness of the Cockney people. Of course come the weekend nights it was either the Good Intent, Bell or the Masons.

Stan and Joyce ran the Good Intent and as a market pub they did a great lunch time trade but never opened till about 8.30 pm at night time, they had a barman called Brian Butters who I got on with very well, Brian was a Millwall supporter and me a Celtic supporter so we had many a good chin wag over the football scene. Brian was live in bar staff so was never late for his shift. Stan the Guvnor seemed to me to always be "miles away". I know Joyce wanted to start a family but I don't think Stan was interested, anyway to be truthful Joyce and Brian "eloped" and got a flat in the Old Kent rd and had a baby daughter which made the two of them very happy, last I heard was Joyce was working in a launderette on the Old Kent rd and Brian was a painter.

Anyway getting back to me living in digs on Cold harbour lane, Fred was the name of the Landlord, he came from Sittingbourne in Kent and was an ex boxer [a bit punch drunk] and when I moved in there I had a room on the top of the house [all my life living in digs it seems 95% of the time the room that I would have would be on the top floor !!]. this Fred was a bit of a pest and as soon as I came home from work he would open his door on the ground floor and come out and want to talk a load of rubbish, so at the end up I just used to brush past him and go up the stairs with him following after me until I had enough one night and told him to "F**k off" and stop annoying me, well it worked thank God.

Opposite my digs were a few shops and a cafe on the corner called Johnny's where I used to have a cup of tea in the morning before starting work on Peter Smiths job. One day it was lashing down with rain, as I got on to the site all the other bricklayers and hoddies [hod carriers] were sitting in the canteen because bricklayers can't build bricks when its raining as the cement would run all down the face of the wall and leave a horrible mess when it dried later.

So we all sat around playing cards but the forecast was for rain all day long, so cut a long story short I went to the Sun and Doves pub in Cold harbour lane at opening time at 11 am and stayed until closing time at 3 in the afternoon and after drinking about eight pints I wanted to go home for a sleep. I went back to my digs and up to my room, went to bed and fell fast asleep.

Next thing it seemed my alarm was going at at 7. 30 am and I got up quickly, thinking I'm going to be late for work, I rushed out my door thinking I can get a quick cup of tea from Johnny's cafe before work but the cafe was closed as was the shops beside it and I thought that's funny!!!!.

Then I looked and people were going in and coming out of the Prince of Wales pub beside me, I was trying to work this out when it dawned on me when my alarm clock went off it wasn't 7.30 in the morning it was 7.30 in the evening. !!!!

What a shock I got but at the same time thought ach what the hell and went into the Prince of Wales pub and had a drink till closing time knowing my head would be a bit fuzzy in the morning but I was in my early twenty's so I would just shrug it off. Yes come the morning and I was up before my alarm went off, had a wash and shave and over to Johnny's cafe for a bacon roll and cuppa tea and on to the site because it wasn't raining today.

When I was working on this site I would always be singing every day as I was building bricks as I'm a happy go lucky person really and it made me feel good as opposed to lots of other bricklayers who would have a long face and be grumpy.

When you worked beside people like that it made a day seem like a week !!. Anyway there was this old bricklayer called Bert who would have been in his early 60's, he worked with the other gang of bricklayers and every day at lunch time he would pass us going to Cold harbour lane to catch the bus down to Camberwell gate where he lived. I said to Bill the bricklayer I was working with "look at that geezer he never smiles and always has a long face" and Bill said to me Danny, Bert's wife's dying and he goes home every lunch time to be with her to see if he can help her.

Oh I felt terrible I had never realised this and it taught me a lesson for later in life that you never knew what trouble a person is going through if they don't smile. I actually got to talk to Bert a few times after this as he would pop into the Rock pub at Camberwell gate where I drank sometimes and he was a nice man really but burdened down with his wife's illness.

One night I finished work and went down to Walworth rd and had a cup of tea and sandwich in one of the cafes there and went down the Lane and had a drink in the Masons then the Bell and finally the Good Intent then I would get the bus back to my digs and buy some fish and chips on the way home or a Chinese take away but that never happened this night because when I went into the Good Intent at 9 pm there was a woman there called Maggie FitzGerald.

Maggie [Maggie Fitz] was sitting at the back of the bar where I usually had a drink with Richie and Andy Storrie and she was the only other person in the pub except Stan the Guvnor who was serving behind the bar.

*[Photo of the Good Intent pub and
a later Guvnor Johnny Clark the ex boxer.]*

So I went over to join Maggie in a drink and remember I had
my working clothes on and big cement boots, never the less I
had saw Maggie a few times before when she had popped into
the Intent or Bells for a quick drink. Maggie had been married
but lived on her own now but cut a long story short we had a
fair few drinks together and when it was closing time I said to
her "are you taking me home for a coffee" ? and she said "yes"
so we started walking back to her home in Liverpool grove
[which was one of those lovely Church commission houses].
Maggie was 40 years old and I was 22 but she was a nice young
looking 40 with a nice figure and good looks and getting back
to her place we had a coffee and then we "cemented our
relationship" that night with me leaving Maggie's house in the
morning and catching the 45 bus from Walworth rd to my
building site at Cold harbour lane with a warm smile on my
face !!

This was the start of our relationship which would last on and
off for six or seven years, I would go down and visit Maggie on
Wednesday nights about seven pm and we'd sit and watch TV
and I would leave at ten thirty, catch the last pint in the Red
Lion pub at Camberwell gate and catch the bus back to my digs.
Then on Friday nights I would finish work at five o'clock, go

back to my digs pay Fred his rent money then have a bath and get suited and booted have something to eat in some cafe and start my Friday night drinking usually in the Horse and Groom pub at the corner of Penrose st/Walworth rd opposite the entrance to the Lane and visit the Masons, Bell and Good Intent. A lady called Joyce ran the Horse and Groom back then. I think her husbands name was Bill ?

Some times Maggie would meet me in the Good Intent as that was the last pub I visited Friday evenings, if not then I would walk round to her place in Liverpool grove and I would stay Friday night, Saturday night and Sunday till about ten pm when I would leave her place, have the last pint in the Red Lion pub and get the bus back to my digs.

To be truthful I couldn't have been happier with this arrangement and life for me was looking good living in South London. Then I had a row with Peter Smith the subcontractor I was working with and told him to shove his job, this happened during the week so I went back on the Friday to pick my money up and fair enough all my money was there because in those days some sub contractors were notorious for "knocking" you for your money.

I heard through the grapevine that they were looking for bricklayers up in Brixton on a massive big housing estate which was on the top end of Coldharbour lane and down Summerleyton rd [in fact this estate was built in different phases and I would work on it on four different occasions over the years]. Sir Lindsey Parkinson's did the 1st phase. Then Fairclough the 2nd phase and finally Sindall's done the 3rd phase.

This really was a massive housing estate and in fact the photo below of "The Barrier block" was the end of the estate, this really was a long block and it went along Cold harbour lane and returned not only into Summerleyton rd one side but also returned on the other side into Moorland rd. When we were building bricks on it there was a Tower crane that was

11

stationary and another Tower crane that was on a railway line [just like a train locomotive] so it could travel up and down the whole length of the block, yes that's how long the block was.

[photo of the Barrier block in Summerleyton rd Brixton].

The first phase of this massive estate had Sir Lindsey Parkinson as the main contractor and Jimmy Young was the sub contract bricklayer, he was an OK guy, one day at breakfast time I was working on the first lift of scaffolding [about 6 feet off the ground] the hod carriers had a couple of scaffold boards from the ground level going up at an angle to the first lift where they could walk up with hods of bricks and mortar. Anyway the shout went up "tea up" and as I walked on to these scaffold boards leading down to the ground they collapsed under me and I fell, the scaffold boards landed on their edge and I fell on them on my side and busted a few of my ribs. Oh what a pain, I never called an ambulance but boy was I in pain.

I had registered with a Doctor called Dr Wetherup, his surgery was in East st opposite The Masons Arms pub and he wrapped crepe bandages round my ribs, he said no work for you for a while lad. I had a week off work and visited The Sun and Doves and Prince of Wales pubs every day. Then I ran out of money and had to go back to work, the subcontractor [or Subby as we called them] put me building just face brick corners, only corners as this saved me walking up and down building the wall. Anyway a week passed and I was a lot better but it was murder trying to get to sleep at night, every time I turned it was sore, so My love life with Maggie at the weekends had to be put on hold I'm afraid. !!!

Anyway soon enough my ribs were back to normal which was a great relief, so I'm working away on this Site at Coldharbour lane, I had started off at getting £8 per shift but we could get bonus if we "speeded up" and being young would love to race to see who could build bricks the fastest [the only one who benefited from this really was the subby as he only paid a small amount of bonus but I didn't mind it always made the day go in faster when you worked hard] Again I was staying with Maggie at the weekends and drinking in the pubs down East st or the pubs just off of it.

Building trade workers back then in the 60's/70s only worked to 1 o'clock on a Saturday and we got paid the full shift, so then it was either have a drink in the pub nearest the site you were working on or in my case I would get the 45 bus from Coldharbour lane and be in the Good Intent pub on East st by 1.30, so still a good hour and half before closing time. On Sunday mornings we changed pubs and the place we met up in was the Lord Camden in Morecambe st just at the back of the Lane. Sid and his wife Brenda ran it and Sid was a character, I remember he always wore a cardigan and when playing someone a game of Shove halfpenny, he would say to his opponent, Cor look at the gorgeous bird passing the door, his opponent would look up and Sid would pull a stick of chalk out of his cardigan pocket and quickly mark down a couple of score marks on the shove halfpenny table and wink at us who saw this happen.

Sunday mornings we Would knock on the Camden's door just after 11 am [remember it was officially 12 noon opening time] and Sid would let us in, There was Richie, Andy Storrie, Davie Sherry, Pat Grimes and a few other Glasgow lads from Blendon row and Paisley Billy [Paisley is a town 7 miles outside of

Glasgow]. It was like Scots corner on a Sunday morning and there was always plenty of laughing and "winding each other up". Although I must say it was Richie who would regale us with story's and jokes, he used to have us rolled up laughing with tears rolling down our faces.

After a while Sid and his wife left the Camden and a new Guvnor called Tony McGillycuddy his wife and dad Len and Mum Nancy took the pub over but nothing changed much, we still got in early on Sunday mornings and had about an hours "afters" after official closing time of 2 o'clock, I clearly remember one Sunday morning and Paisley Billy came in to the Camden all dressed in Denim, Denim jeans, Denim shirt and Denim jacket and wearing a pair of black shiny pointed boots !!!! well the Micky taking started right away, "bloody hell Billy you look like a Cowboy" said one of the lads and Richie chimed in "Oh yeah I saw Billy trying to Lasso an Alsatian dog in East st this morning" and every time Billy said anything everybody would say "yup pardner" and a few lads would start singing "Rawhide" it really was a great craic in the Camden on Sundays.

Then some Sunday afternoons we would all take a trip over to Johnny Lyman's pub the Gladstone in King and Queen st, which was only a few minutes walk away and it was always packed and again we got a late drink if we wanted too. Johnny Lyman would be sitting in his "music booth" with his headphones on and playing LP records like Frank Sinatra etc it was great. Legend has it, and it has been verified by lots of people who were there, that late one night the pub was in full swing and again Johnny was in his "music booth" when a young Copper walked into the pub, asked who the Guvnor was, then walked over and said to John "Have you any idea what the time is" John replied "Ain't got a clue babe" the young Policeman said "it's 2 o'clock in the morning" and Johnny replied with "My how time flies in when you're enjoying yourself". the Copper said "right everyone out of the pub right now" and to John said "I will inform my chief Inspector in Carter street police station first thing in the morning" and John said "Send him my best regards he's a friend of mine" from that day on that young Copper was never seen patrolling the streets of Walworth again. !!!!

[A photo of Johnny Lyman's pub "The Gladstone" in King and Queen st. "With Chic the barman"]

The years were flying in and it was 1972, I was still working on that big estate in Coldharbour lane and by this time Maggie had been transferred form her Church commission house in Liverpool grove to just 5 minutes walk away to number 8 Burton Grove [top floor] which had been refurbished and Maggie now had a bathroom with a bath in it and she asked me did I want to move in with her full time and I said yes [mistake], so I left my digs behind me in Coldharbour lane and said goodbye to old Fred my Landlord, the first couple of months were good living with Maggie and then I got to "losing" a bit of my freedom and worse than that Maggie had a son [a cardboard gangster] called Jimmy Fitz who never wanted to work a day in his life and Maggie bought a put me up bed for him in the front room.

Maggie was a sister in law to Frankie Fraser the South London gangster and her son tried to make out that because Frankie Fraser was his Uncle it made him a gangster but the guy was a complete waster and not many people had time for him at all. I

15

offered to get him a job as a hod carrier but he wasn't interested. This was causing friction between Maggie and me but I also understand that blood is thicker than water and after all he was her son.

There had been a change to the income tax laws for the building trade and self employed bricklayers were now stopped exactly one third of our wages because it used to be all cash payments beforehand and you should have settled up your tax bill with the tax man every April but loads of building trade workers who were self employed never did and the tax man was losing millions of pounds each year.

So a new scheme came out it was called a "714" tax exemption certificate, basically anyone in the building trade who was self employed could apply for and get one of these "714's" it was like a cheque book and had 52 pages on it and each page covered one complete week.

When you got your "714" you would produce it on a Friday night to the guvnor who was paying you your cash and he would sign the amount of cash he had paid you and he wouldn't stop you a third of your wages, you in turn would give him the page for his tax records and you would have the stub just like a cheque book for your tax records, sounded good but it turned out to be one of the biggest tax fiddles ever going. !!!

See when you got your "714" book you could say to the tax man you had lost it or it was stolen and you would get issued with a new one, the "old lost one" then could be used to sign for a huge amount of money say a couple of thousand pounds by a greedy sub contractor and he would get off Scot free for that amount of money at the end of the tax year.

You had some guys would go on the site and make a deal with the sub contractor and for talking sake say all the wages came to £2 thousand pounds this person would let the Subby sign the 2 Grand on his ticket and charge everyone on site 10 % so he would make £200 just with that one ticket and the Subby was in the clear as as the holder of the "714" ticket was responsible for all this money [but he had already told the tax man this ticket was stolen or lost so he couldn't be held accountable for it].

A few years down the line the tax man would change these "714's" to a a small card with the owners photo and National insurance number etc so it would be foolproof and the fiddle would end but it took about 3 years for the tax man to hit on the right method of card to use. While in those 3 years some people made a fortune out of these "714's" and some even retired to Spain. !!!!

- - - - -

Chapter 2

The Heygate Estate

Anyway I have to say I was always legitimate because when these "714's" first came out I started working direct on my cards, paid my weekly tax and National Insurance stamps and the first person I started with doing this was Dave Sullivan who was the brickwork subcontractor for the Heygate estate at the Elephant and Castle. I started working on the building of the Heygate in April 1972 and I worked alongside his works partner Roy Motram who lived round the Elephant and we had loads of red brick boundary walls to build and all the brickwork on the garages, there was so much work there for us bricklayers, there were numerous different bricklaying gangs there. Roy and me, then Johnny O'Neil and Paddy Marks and big Tosh then Manchester Roy and Irish John and Jimmy etc. Roy and me also built every brick and block on the Crossway Mission hall on the Heygate.

[Marston block on the Heygate on Deacon way looking down to the Crossway Mission hall and the New Kent rd.]

Working on the Heygate estate was great, we had so much brickwork to build just look at the photo above and you can see the red brick walls. Dave Sullivan was a great Subby to work for and every Friday he would draw up in his old Rover 90 car and pull out a chamois leather bag full of twenty, ten, five and £1 notes. Remember it was only a year since we had went decimal and when Dave paid you out [he had already measured up your brickwork built for that week] he would say "right under 50 pence its mine and over 50 pence its yours". He would have his little calculator with him and work out what your wages were and if your wages came to [after tax] £48. 25 pence he would only pay you £48. but if your money came to £48.62 pence then he would pay you £49.

Dave also had other men employed on the Heygate, they would be erecting the internal partition walls of all the flats. When every concrete floor was completed the Tower cranes would position these internal partition wall units on the concrete slab. They were story height lightweight breeze block units, so about 8 feet 5 inch tall and 3 feet wide. The Carpenter would come in to each flat and drill a metal channel onto the ceiling which these story height units would slot into obviously leaving out door openings.

The guys working for Dave would slot these units into the channels, use a spirit level to make sure they were erect[plumb] and there would be about an inch gap at the bottom which the guys would put wooden wedges under so they could move them about to make sure they were plumb, then fill in the inch gap with a type of polyfilla. Now the brainwave of the Architect was these units were smooth so they didn't have to be plastered over, each unit butted against each other [3 feet sections wide] and the guys buttered a polyfilla on the edge so when they butted to each other there was no space, and any excess polyfilla was sandpapered down. These unit walls were now ready for the residents when they moved in to paste wallpaper on them right away. This saved building traditional breeze block walls, then getting them plastered over and then clearing

19

all the mess up after, I think it was a brilliant idea and every room had all these units dropped off by the tower cranes so they were already there and didn't have to be manhandled up on the platform hoists into every room. It was so time saving and just one reason how the Heygate was built so quickly and ready for tenants to move in just after starting work on it 3 years previously.

Unfortunately one of the precast concrete cladding workers who helped guide these cladding units into their position as the tower crane lowered them down, fell from the 3rd floor as he was guiding one of the concrete units into its place. His name was Bernie and he was a Yorkshire lad, he suffered brain damage but could still get about and John Laing the main contractor of the Heygate gave him a job for life [but not with the concrete cladding units obviously] he would just be sweeping out the canteen and stores on site. He could speak but it was impaired poor lad.

This was 1972 and the time of the building trade workers strike and lots of building sites in London were closed down and not allowed to open as there would be pickets at the gates and some had pick axe handles to intimidate you from going into work, although the Heygate was deliberately kept open so the workers there could contribute money each week to the unions. And at a later date in 1974 we had the 3 day working week but that never affected us bricklayers as we had a cement mixer that was run on diesel.

Come every Friday I would go for a pint and a ham or cheese roll when I worked on the construction of the Heygate, it all depended what part of the Heygate I was working on to which pub I used, it could have been the Rose and Crown, or the Archduke Charles or the County terrace tavern but this particular Friday I used the Hampton Court Palace pub in Hampton st ran by Tom Reidy and his wife Dolly.

[Photo of the Hampton Court palace pub in Hampton st/Crampton st.]

Anyway I walks into the Hampton court on this Friday and orders a pint and ham roll and was served by Tom the Guvnor who was a bit of a character, him and his wife Dolly ran a great pub and had plenty of live music and great singers over the years including Dorothy Squires [who was once married to actor Roger Moore]. So I'm having a pint and this young KP peanut and crisp salesman walks in and goes over to Tom and says "I want paying for last months crisps and peanuts".

Tom looks at him and says "so you want paying for last month young man do you, well let me tell you that every month my wife Dolly and me write down all the people that we owe money too, put their names on slips of paper and put them in a hat and the lucky one drawn out of the hat gets paid. But you "Ya Plonker" your names not even in the bloody hat". Exit one very embarrassed young KP peanut salesman. Tom and Dolly moved away and later Dolly died and Tom ended up in a men's hostel at Vauxhall bridge such a shame they were a nice couple.

Of course later John and Mauraa would take over the Hampton and made it into a brilliant pub, he was a great governor and nothing was a problem for John, he would always help you if he could. I heard the he and Maura split up, she went back home to

21

Ireland and John sadly passed away but they will always be remembered by all the people round the Elephant and Walworth with great fondness. My ex-wife Mo worked there as a barmaid when John and Maura had it.

I have to tell you a story about the Crossway Mission hall, as I say Roy Motram and myself built every brick and block on it with the help of our hod carrier Arthur Morgan. One day Roy and me were building brickwork on the outside walls of the caretakers house and our next move was once we reached scaffold height [5 feet high] we would go inside and build the internal block work walls. Anyway the Site agent on the Crossway was called Jack and he was a bricklayer by trade too. He said to Roy and me "I'll get my chalk line and ping a chalk line down for you for the first course of blocks onto the concrete floor to save you a bit of time", we said you don't have to Jack but he insisted so we let him carry on.

So we went in and started building the block walls to Jack's chalk line, then every other block wall we measured off of the course of blocks that we built to Jacks chalk line. Cut a long story short we had finished building the Caretakers house which was ground level and one story high. The carpenter had came in after we had built all the internal block walls up to floor joist height, laid out his wooden joists and all the walls below carried on upwards on top of the walls built below so there was no need to measure anything we just followed the walls below and built on top of them.

One day when coming back from breakfast Roy said to me look inside the Caretakers house don't those walls look off square? and sure thing yes they did look out of square, how can this be. Well we went and measured the wall at one end that Jack had chalk lined out for us and measured it at the other end and it was 4 inches out of square, when he measured for the chalk line he had made the oldest mistake in the book and went to the wrong side one end and that made all the walls out of square as we had measured off the first wall.

"Bloody hell" I said all the block-work will have to come down, that's every wall ground floor and first floor. Anyway we went and told Jack the bad news and he said no its your fault you must have went to the wrong side of my chalk line, so went and cleared the mortar away on the first course of blocks and it showed we had followed Jack's chalk line. He went ashen white and started calling himself all the names under the sun but the proof of the pudding was all the walls would have to be pulled down and the Wooden joists would have to be propped up as they had been built into the walls either end.

I think Jack wanted to commit suicide, poor man. Anyway the main site agent for the Heygate Leo Berry was told about it and they decided to get a gang of labourers in at the weekend and pull every bit of blockwork down and get skips in to take the rubble away and also get a couple of carpenters in to prop up all the joists. This was done over the weekend and Roy and myself had to build all the internal block walls up again but this time to the right measurements.

The Contracts manager Steve Woodlands had to be told about this too and what happened was that the "loss of all the money" was spread down to other parts of the Heygate construction and no one was any the wiser, of course it was awkward for us trying to build the walls back up again with props all over the place but two days later we had finished it and that is an untold story about the Crossway mission hall that hardly a soul in the world knew about [until I typed it up here in my book].

I was still having a drink down the Lane at weekends and it was always good to meet up with your mates at the weekends too, although I had a lot of Cockney mates too by now and as I said before I liked the South London Cockneys. I would walk into the Bell [Royal Albert] in the Lane and Johnny Leonard would be in the saloon bar and when I walked in he would always shout out "hello cousin" and George the Guvnor behind the bar would always greet me with "hello brother", see I told you it was a family pub.!!.

It was quite common in those days for people to have Monday off work [Monday club] and with the Lane not being open Mondays a few of the stall owners would meet up in the Good Intent, Bell or Masons and have a drink till closing time at 3 o'clock but by then they were only getting the "flavour" and I was there on a few Mondays too and then having the "taste" we'd get a mini cab over to either the Log cabin or A&R both drinking clubs which were over the West end of London and drink there till about 8 pm and then a mini cab back to the Lane and carry on drinking till closing time.

Andy Storrie came a few times too and if we landed back in the Bell or Masons Andy would get the "spoons" out and rattle them off his arms and knees to the records being played in the pub and he was good. Andy had a lot of grief in his life and his young son died in the 70s also he got divorced but I have to say Andy was the innocent party in this, out of respect for Andy I wont say anymore but it speaks volumes when his other son Neil and daughter Lesley stayed with their Dad.

[I got to meet up with Andy's son Neil and daughter Lesley later when I was 58 years old]

The Masons arms was always a busy pub and sometimes at weekends have live music and big Davie Sherry was prone to going up and blasting a song out, there was never a dull moment in the Masons and when you were sitting in there during the day you had all the "Hoisters" who come in with all kinds of meat they had lifted from the supermarkets nearby and sell it at a give away price and they always sold whatever they had as people like a bargain.

Big Chase Lived in Blendon row just round the corner from the Masons, he was a carpenter by trade but gave it up as he could make more money at "hoisting". They reckon he was brilliant and if you wanted a new suit of clothes he would take your measurements, then off to the West end or wherever and bring you back your suit and other peoples too. Blendon row seemed to have got a "bad name" over the years but I thought the people were all sound, Georgie and Grace Brindle, Kevin Barry, Paisley Billy and all my fellow Glaswegians etc, the building might have have been run down with old age but the people were good.

[Photo of Blendon row.]

One thing I liked about East st was all the hustle and bustle of people all looking at the different stalls to get a bargain or on Sunday morning down the Lane getting a hot or cold glass of sarsaparilla off of George who had his stall there for years and there was always Maries and other cafes but I have to say my favourite was Arments pie and mash shop in Westmoreland rd and when I first used it in the very early 70s it was on the opposite site of the road from where it is now. If my stomach was a bit squeezy on a Saturday morning from the beer the night before then Pie and mash with liquor seemed to settle my tummy oh and then back into the pub again ha ha.

I used to remember using the Kings Head pub on Walworth rd/Manor place early 70's and it was owned by a guy called Hughie Monaghan from Ireland, Hughie used to be a lorry driver and scrimped and saved enough money over the years so he could buy the tenancy of the Kings Head and him and his wife Beattie [Bridget - Theresa = BT] realised that dream in the late 1960s when they moved into the pub, at that time there were two bars = the Public bar and then the Saloon bar.

In the Saloon bar late 60s and early 70s he had a Go-Go dancer dancing to records and this was very popular with all the males using the pub, later he would have a DJ called King John dressed in a designer suit who would play all the hit records of the day which again pulled the punters in and I was one of them. [By the way the Go Go dancer was King John's girlfriend.] It was a mixed pub Cockney, Irish and Scots all congregating there and Hughie kept a great pub although on a personal point I thought he could be a wee bit sarcastic. Though I will give Hughie credit as every Christmas eve he would open the pub up at 7 pm and it was a completely free bar for all the customers, yes you never paid for one drink the whole night long and this just showed you how much money the pub made all year round which belittled his nickname of "The Miser".

Christina [Gannon] was one of the barmaids there and was always on the ball and she and 47 of us all went to New York from the Kings Head for St Patrick's day celebrations all organized by Hughie. Christina moved back to Galway got married and now has a family of her own.

[Photo of the Kings Head pub on Walworth rd/Manor place.]

I have to say that over the years the Kings Head pub had plenty of characters drinking in it like, The Weasel, The Growler, Gabby John, Andy the Butcher, the Bouncer, The road runner etc. The Bouncers name was Billy Fitzgerald and he got his nickname as he used to be a bouncer on the door of the Shamrock Irish dance hall near Keyworth st at the Elephant and Castle years ago. He was a general builder and had loads of men working for him at one time. Especially when he refurbished all the house along Camberwell new rd either late 70's or early-mid 80s. he was a giant of a man about 6feet four tall ad weighing 25 stones but very softly spoken. At the height of making his money he drank in the Kings head every night and stayed in the Russell Hotel at Russel sq at Euston at £400 per week !!. I remember he used to challenge people that he could drink a pint faster than they could drink a short, He would have a pint of Guinness on the bar and his "challenger" would have a gin and tonic water or vodka and coke and when Hughie behind the bar said "go" the Bouncer raised his pint to his mouth and it was gone in seconds. I never saw him lose a challenge.

The Mad Axe Man

Don O'Leary was from Kerry and his son had an argument with Hughie one Sunday lunch time and Hughie laughed at him as he barred him. So comes Sunday evening and 7 o'clock opening time Don comes into the bar, walks up to Hughie and says you barred my son and laughed didn't you, well Don pulled an axe from under his coat and with all his might embedded it into the top of the bar counter and said well you're not laughing now are you and at this moment I think Hughie ran up the stairs, mind you I don't blame him. Hughie had to get a guy in the following morning to get the bar counter repaired and French Polished.

Manor place baths was just along a bit from the Kings Head in Manor place and early 70s I used to go there and have a hot bath with my pal Richie from Blendon row, we used to have a drink in the Good Intent then go to the Kings Head for the last

27

hour on a Saturday afternoon and off for a hot bath. It was also a venue for boxing and wrestling matches and a few times I went there to watch the wrestling and TV favourites Mick McManus, Johnny Kwango and the Royal brothers would hold our attention on these mid-week bouts and afterwards a walk down to The Duke of Clarence pub on the corner of Manor place/Penton place and have a pint after the wrestling was finished.

Just up from the Duke of Clarence and almost opposite Manor place baths was a fish and chip shop, they sold great fish n chips but they would never sell a portion of chips on its own ?, the people who owned it were real miserable and never smiled especially the woman and this put people that lived near by to avoid it. I have always believed when you run a business dealing directly with people you must be pleasant otherwise people will take their custom elsewhere as they did with this fish and chip shop. What makes people like this so miserable. One last thing about the Kings head pub after I think it was 30 years Hughie handed the pub over to his son Paul. Who got wide screen TV's in to show all the different sports and was doing well until he later tried to take the pub in a different direction selling food and I'm afraid it didn't take off and sadly closed down. Paul had worked hard and it was sad to see him close the pub.

[Manor Place baths in all its glory]

28

I actually have to make a confession about one night when I was in the Kings head pub, remember me telling you about the girl who worked in the site canteen on Peter Smiths job at Colharbour lane [yes the one that always flirted with me]. Anyway at this time I was "living in sin" with Maggie Fitz in Burton grove just off of Portland st and she happened to go down her caravan at Clacton for a weeks holiday which left me on my own.

I was having a drink in the Masons arms East st on the Friday night early about 6 pm and Maggie was due home the following day [Saturday], so I'm having a drink in the Masons and one of the bricklayers who worked on Peter Smiths job happened to walk in to the pub by chance, Tony Perkins was his name and we had a few drinks together. He was still working on Peter Smiths job building all the external walls as the flats by this time had all been built, cut a long story short he said remember "Betty" and I said "yes" well he said she had given Tony her home phone number to give to me if he ever saw me.

I said right away "Oh no I'm living with Maggie" but after a few more drinks a combination of alcohol and lust started taking over I'm ashamed to say I started thinking about "Betty", we left the Masons pub and headed over to Walworth rd and went into the Kings Head to listen to the records being played by "King John" the DJ.

Then after a few more drinks I said to Tony "give me her phone number", I phoned her up and said did she fancy a drink?, she actually lived out at Penge and got a mini cab straight away and was in the Kings Head in half an hour and standing beside me, we had a few drinks [by this time I had thrown all caution to the wind as the alcohol took over] and I said are you inviting me home for a coffee and she said yes.

We caught a black taxi in Walworth rd and half an hour later was in her house out at Penge and coffee was the last thing on both of our minds. We ended up in bed for a night of passion

29

and first thing in the morning too. Betty said to me, "you can come and live with me and just give me £30 a week", bloody hell I was only giving Maggie £15 a week [as that was all she wanted] I said to Betty I would give her a phone next week but I never would.

Then I realised Maggie was coming home that day and I had to rush back to make the bed up, I got the number 12 bus from Penge back down to Walworth rd [no taxi this time, ha ha] I had a couple of drinks in the Bell in the Lane and went home to Maggie's place and she arrived about an hour later. She was feeling a bit "frisky" so we ended up in the bed I had recently made up and oh la la, well I was 25 years old and full of stamina but just hoped that Maggie wouldn't hear through the grapevine that someone had spotted me in the Kings Head with Betty.

I'm honestly ashamed of myself for doing that to Maggie but this is what happened and its all part of my life story, so I have to tell it the way my life unfolded.

One thing I loved about South London and Walworth in particular was there were pubs everywhere and I paid a visit to almost all of them. I remember the Cricketers pub at Newington/Kennington.

[Photo of the Cricketers pub at Newington/Kennington]

The Cricketers when I used it was from early 70s to perhaps late 80s, big Tom Valentine was the Guvnor and ran a great pub, he had live music bands in the saloon bar weekend nights and had a packed public bar during the week mainly of building trade workers who would have their own little groups for playing cards.

There was another thing that Tom done and that was to change cheques for building trade workers, there wasn't many building trade workers who had bank accounts in the early 70s. It used to be always cash in our wage packets back then but there were a few Sub contractors who started to pay with cheques as a few of them had been robbed at gunpoint when they paid cash.

What Tom done was made sure of the name of the sub contractor paying the cheques were all legal, when he had that sorted out then what he done on a Friday night when the cheques were handed over was take the cheque and put it into his safe upstairs but wouldn't pay the guy his money for a few hours so he at least got about 4 or 5 pints worth of money off them and then he would pay them their cash. Remember it was illegal to charge 5% or 10% or any percentage if you didn't declare this money to the tax/v.a.t. man. [Some publicans did this and were turned over by the tax man]

I remember one Friday night and this guy came in when I was having a pint in the public bar and he held Tom a cheque, Tom took it no problem and after about 2 hours came down with the guys money and the guy started shouting more than half my money is missing and Tom held him a cheque he had held in to Tom about a year previously and it had bounced. Needless to say that guy never used the Cricketers again. Tom had a few of those cheques that had "bounced" and he had them in a drawer upstairs just ready for that person to come into his pub again, he had a retentive memory did Tom.

There was another thing the punters in the Cricketers liked and that was on a Sunday morning from about 9.30 am you could

31

get into the pub via Kennington lane so no one would notice you going in, remember official opening time on a Sunday was 12 noon back then and some Sunday mornings the public bar was packed from 10.am onwards. Of course the Cops were no fools they knew what pubs were doing "earlys or afters" but as long as they never called to a pub to sort out any fighting then they would turn a "blind eye" to this.

I never really drank that much in Kennington but I had a few drinks along Manor place at the Kennington end of Walworth, there were two pubs with almost the same name, The Surrey view and the Surrey garden arms, I think I have got their names right ? oh and the Duke of Sutherland pub on Lorrimore rd and the Faunce

[Photo of the Duke of Sutherland pub on Lorrimore rd Se 17]

I remember one night I had a drink in the Tankard pub on the corner of Walworth rd and Amelia st, I was with John Orr [Ginger John] Pat Carney, Billy the Weasel and Patsy Carroll we left the Tankard and went along Amelia st a few yards to the Queens Head pub and had a drink in there. Ginger John had a great singing voice and after we had got a pint in our hands John started singing, it was great or so we thought until the Guvnor [a stand in manager] said "no singing allowed in this pub, right your barred" he said to John and we looked on in amazement, we started to say "its only a song what harm can it do" and then he said "you're all barred too", I said "why are were barred too when were not singing" ?

"No" he said "but you're all listening"!!!!. John had just recently came out of prison for GBH so we all grabbed John and bundled him out the door otherwise he would have killed the guy. We ended up in the Bell in East st that night in the public bar and John was in great voice and no one complained, in fact George the Guvnor bought us all a drink.

Just as a matter of fact did you know how the Bell pub got its name ? its proper name was the Royal Albert but years and years ago there used to be a bell fixed to the wall of the pub and when the market was ready to open or close the bell was rang.

Of course when I had landed in South London in 1969 to live and work there were lots more pubs but lots were being demolished to make way for the Aylesbury, Heygate and Salisbury housing estates and terraced houses that generations of people grew up in were being demolished slowly but surely.

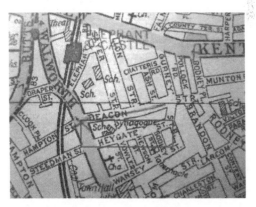

[Photo of Heygate st and the surrounding streets of which many are long gone now, many of these streets as I say have now disappeared but some have retained their names but I wonder for how long.]

33

In fact I had never heard of places like Vowler st, Gurney st, Ash st, Lion st, etc etc until I joined a Walworth facebook group ran by Darren Lock [Admin] and saw a street map of the names of streets that would be later demolished to make way for the Heygate estate. It must sadden people of that generation that the homes their family and their descendants grew up in were being bulldozed. That's why I think its good to document names of streets and people so they're not lost forever and photos to refresh peoples memories and I hope I have done this in my book. With the passing of time slowly but surely names of pubs, shops, streets will only be remembered if they are mentioned in books/historical documents, how many of us can remember back say a few generations or so, it's hard, eh.

[Photo above of Ray Dennis Johnson's Mum and Dad sitting in the Prince Albert pub at the bottom of their street and his Mum holding Ray as a baby in Vowler street where they all lived, Mum sitting with Baby Ray outside their home. Ray now lives over in Australia.]

I had been working on another job for Dave Sullivan, sometimes he would take me off the building of the Heygate and transfer me to a job he had down at Blackfriars but the south side of Blackfriars bridge and right on the edge of the River Thames, it was another massive site with hundreds of new flats being built and an office block which was 34 stories tall. [tallest office block in London at the time]

My job was to get the brickwork and blockwork going so when other bricklayers came after me they would know what the layout was. There was only a weeks work on each floor of brickwork, it was just solid brickwork on one side of the lift shaft [this was the express lift] and then three solid brick piers on the side of the slow lift, which allowed two lift doors for the slow lift. Then some blockwork to be built in the Gents and Ladies toilets. Dave gave me another bricklayer and a hod carrier to work with me. All the bricks and blocks had been previously left on each floor by the tower crane. So all my hod carrier had to do was use the cement mixer on the ground floor and fill his barrows up and take them up on one of the two service hoists.

Dave sent down two of his men who had been working on the Heygate estate putting up the internal partition walls, those solid "breeze" units which you could wallpaper over straight away, anyway they were two brothers Damian and Raymond Flanagan and they had never built a brick or block in their life so I showed them how to do it and eventually the two of them turned out to be good bricklayers and friends with me.

The good thing about this office block was the glazier had put the glass in all the first four floors so no wind coming through the building but after the 4th floor there was no glass in the window openings and even on a "calm" day the wind would whistle through there and freeze you, so I got Dave to transfer me to one of his other jobs. !!!

The year was now 1974 and the time of the 3 day working week, when we had electric power cuts at any time. I remember standing in the Horse and Groom pub at Walworth rd/Penrose st one night and we had a power cut but Bill and Joyce who ran the pub had candles all at the ready, which were lit up and I spoke to one Cockney lad who would have been well into his 70's and he said to me this is what it was like during the blitz in WW 2 son and because of this people would all start chatting to each other as we had a "common enemy" and it was like this with the power cuts we all started chatting to each other.

I'm afraid Maggie Fitz and me were having lots of rows, I would come home from work some days and Maggie had been to one of the pubs down East st and invited people back for a drink in her house. I would come in from work and it was like a party, I don't blame the people as I knew most of them but between that and her "carboard gangster" son living there Maggie and me parted company, I wished her good luck but enough was enough for me.

I had saved up about £800 while living with Maggie, I was 26 years old and thought to myself right I'm going to Australia, I went up to Glasgow to see my Ma and Da and up there I paid for a single air ticket to Sydney, got my inoculations done and passport and flew off into the sunset thinking what will Oz be like, well Danny boy only one way to find out. !!

I wont mention my 2 years of living there here as I want all the chapters of my book in Part 1 to be about living in South London but I do mention it in Part 2 at the very end of my book What I will say is after a bad start things got good until I met this New Zealand girl Trudy whom I would live with, I was in two car crashes, My NZ girlfriend **tried to murder me** [honestly] while I was sleeping in our flat in Melbourne but survived to live to tell the tale and came back to South London and Walworth 2 years later with £4.000 in my pocket and just in time for the long hot summer of 1976.

- - - - -

Chapter 3

Back in Walworth Again

Well I landed back first of all In Glasgow to see my Ma and Da and gave them a nice few quid and then a week later got a train from Glasgow central to London Euston and back to London, I booked into the Royal Scot hotel at £20 per night and for the next two weeks it was wine, women and song as I tried my best to spend the remaining £3.000 as fast as I could. They had this thing called a "chef master" in my hotel room and it had six compartments in it , one had a half bottle of Vodka, the others were Gin, Scotch etc and beer [chilled] They had to restock my "chef master" twice in the first week and I wasn't short of female companionship either lol.

I was always giving a "backhander" to the head wine waiter and the Maitre De and of course the doorman and when I walked into the Hotel it was always Good day Mr Gill or how are you Mr Gill as another £5 note was slipped to them. Lord and Lady Muck could have been living there but I was treated like Royalty. My money was going fast but I have no regrets whatsoever I loved the "Millionaires" life style, of course I knew it wouldn't last for ever but boy did I enjoy it. Then I took a trip over to South London and met up with all my old pals down East st and Walworth, I had a drink with Richie and Andy Storrie and a few of my Cockney mates and then I bumped into Maggie Fitz in the street and like a fool I agreed to go back and live with her !!.

I said goodbye to the Royal Scot hotel and I think they were sorry to see me go, I moved back in with Maggie and out of my remaining money bought her a gold bracelet with "Danny&Maggie xx" inscribed on it and she lost it the very first day she put it on to go to work. Well I think that was a "bad omen" but such is life, at least Maggie's son the "cardboard gangster" wasn't there any more so I was grateful for that. I rang up Dave Sullivan my old Guvnor and said "have you any work on" ? Dave said "yes I'm finishing off a Job at Portland st [just round the corner from Maggie's house in Burton grove] its the new Michael Faraday school" so with my new tool-bag and new tools and new spirit level I turned up at the Michael Faraday school for an 8 o'clock start on the Monday morning.

[Photo of ex Michael Faraday school footballers taken in 1956. From back row left to right: Johnny Norris, Paul Austin, and Peter Emery, Bottom row left to right. John Cordrey, Les Allen and Peter Adams.]

So I started work on the new Michael Faraday school and was working with another two bricklayers but they weren't from Walworth and to be truthful I never took to them, they wanted to know why I had left Australia [because I was so sun-tanned] and come back to London and I answered them saying because I love living in South London especially the Walworth/Elephant area. We went to the Bricklayers arms at Westmoreland rd for a lunch time pint and I was talking to a few people that I knew because these other two bricklayers didn't want to know me. I only stayed working on the Michael Farady school for a week

38

and left Dave Sullivan as I heard they were looking for bricklayers up at Brixton on that massive estate I had previously worked on at the top of Coldharbour lane. Remember this was just the start of the long hot summer of 1976 and we had constant sunshine for four months solid. I was wearing shorts and a T shirt [this is what I wore when I lived in Oz] because it was stifling hot you couldn't wear long trousers well not it this heat.

[Photo of the houses being built inside the barrier block at Coldharbour lane, Brixton]

I got to know a good few of the bricklayers on this massive estate, in fact I think there were 20 of us bricklayers there and about 8 hod carriers, Tony and Fred were the brickwork sub contractors there. Tony was a loud mouth whereas Fred was quieter and nicer but the two of them were "money mad" and I remember I had been working there for about three days when this Tony came over and started shouting at us of how he wanted a good face brick job done and done quickly, I said to him "listen you might talk to the other [younger] bricklayers like that but don't speak to me like that". He said oh no I didn't mean you mate as I have been watching you mate and you're a good bricklayer, at least we now knew where we stood and he never "mouthed off" at me again. John Quinnliven was the foreman bricklayer there and he was a good guy.

One day sitting in the canteen at breakfast time the union rep came into the canteen and said how many bricklayers here are in the union and one guy held his hand up, the union rep started shouting "I have been lied to" I have been told every bricklayer on site is in the union, anyway cut a long story short Tony and Fred the Guvnors took him into the site office and a "deal" was struck up because the union rep never came back. This Tony and Fred were making loads of money on this site and didn't want it closed down with a building strike.

When I finished work at night time I got the 45 bus at Gresham rd outside our site and got it down to Walworth rd and would get into the Rock pub at 5.30 pm opening time and have two pints and be back at Maggie's place for my dinner at 6.30 pm. I wouldn't go out after that until the weekend and then it was Friday night, Saturday night and Sundays, Maggie would come out with some Saturday nights, yes I have always liked a drink but also worked hard.

Then disaster, Maggie's son Jimmy Fitz the "cardboard gangster" must have got thrown out of wherever he was living and she put him up again, well this caused lots of "aggro" between Maggie and me.

This lasted till about the end of September and then I saw an advert for bricklayers wanted in West Germany in the evening standard newspaper and I thought oh what the hell, so I jacked in Tony and Fred's job at Brixton. I told them I was having "women trouble" and was heading off to Germany to live and work and the two of them said "if you come back and are looking for the start then come back to us no probs".
So I had my final drink in the Good Intent pub that Friday night with Richie and a few of the other boys and come Saturday morning the mini cab I had ordered came to Burton grove at 9 am and myself, suitcase, tool bag and level were off to Charing cross railway station where we met this guy called John Fox or "Foxy" and he put us all on the train going to Harwich I think ? then caught the sea ferry over to Holland.

Again I won't tell my story of going to Germany as I want my book to mainly to be about South London and my adventures and lifetime there but what I will say is it was one disaster after the other and the biggest disaster was being stranded at Ramsgate [when the people I lived with in Germany had driven us back for a long weekend] I was destitute, but the full story will be told in Part 2 at the end of my book].

So five months after leaving for West Germany I was back in South London with no money, no digs, no tools or level and no passport and a wiser man. Fair play to my pal Richie him and his wife Beryl they put me in their council house just off the bottom end of Coldharbour lane [Denmark hill end]. It was a Sunday night when Richie took me in and he gave me a few quid to tide me over until I started work. On the Monday morning I got the bus up to Brixton to Tony and Fred's job and the first person I saw was John Quinnliven the foreman bricklayer and he started me there and then, I said I have no tools John [I said its a long story and I will tell you later] anyway John borrowed a brick trowel, spirit Level and brick hammer etc from other brickies there, gave them to me and I started work at 8 am.

I told John "I needed paying that week right up to the Friday nigh" [so I could have money to get digs and pay a week in advance] He said "no probs". Living at Richie and Beryls I went out looking for digs and saw in a newsagents window there was an advert for a room in St Giles rd Camberwell. So I went down to look at the room in St Giles rd and lets call them "Barry and Matilda" they were a Nigerian couple and they said yes they had a room down in the basement, I looked at it and it was the usual, bed, table and two chairs, a wardrobe and chest of drawers that you have in most digs. I took it straight away and told them I would move in on Friday night coming, but never realising **all that would happen** to me in my stay there which will make you the reader either laugh or cry.

[Photo showing my basement flat in St Giles rd
to the left hand side]

I thanked Richie and Beryl for all their help they had given me and after work went straight to my new digs and paid the £12 a week rent and a deposit of £12 to Matilda, I was getting paid £18 per shift at Tony and Fred's so minus the tax I had over £75 so happy days once again. I went out to celebrate in the local pubs the Orange tree, Bricklayers arms and the Flying Dutchman. Life was looking good again for me. It was now February and a bit chilly but after a few beers after work I would take a Chinese take away or fish n chips back with me to my digs and after finishing that read a book and go to bed.

One night I remember I finished work had something to eat in a cafe at Camberwell and got a bus down to the Elephant and went to one of the cinemas there to watch the horror film **Carrie,** [with Linda Blair] what a scary bloomin movie !!!. so anyway I made my way back to my digs in St Giles rd, it was late so I went to bed I was cold as it was still February, anyway I pulled the bed sheets over me to get warm as there was no heating in my room. I was just dozing off to sleep when there was this awful sound C-R-E-E-K, the wardrobe door opened all on its own, Arghh !!!! after watching the horror film Carrie an hour or so ago I thought it was her hiding in my wardrobe [isn't it terrible the things that go through your mind] I jumped up out of bed and ran over to the wardrobe while pulling the other door open but no sign of "Carrie" thank God. Of course it was because of the cold of February that the wood of the door contracted and made it come open but what a bloomin fright. !!

So life for me was good, working up at the barrier block estate in Brixton and having a few beers after work then going down the Lane at the weekends to meet up with my pals. One Saturday night I came back to my digs ad went to bed and fell asleep when about 3 am my bedroom door opened and it was Matilda dressed in her nightie and she said to me "can you do me a favour", well I was all ears until she said to me "can you loan me £10 saying although she was still married to Barry they never slept together and he never gave her any money", in fact they were going to get divorced, anyway I gave Matilda £10 and she leaned over and kissed me but then like a shot was out of my room.

The following week I was in my room about nine o'clock in the evening I think it was a Tuesday night and I was laying on top of my bed reading a book when Matilda knocked on my door saying "its me". I got up and opened the door and she came into the room and said "do you like music" ? I answered "yes", she said "I have a small radio would you like to have it" and I said yes. Matilda said "I like listening to music on the radio so perhaps I can come down to your room and we can listen to the music together", [Oh, Yes,Yes,Yes.] oh I said "that's a good idea and tell me do you like a drink" and she said "I love Bacardi". Well I thought Danny boy your luck's in son, I said to her "I'll bring home a bottle of Bacardi tomorrow night and we can listen to the music together" [and maybe make music together too I thought !!].

So that was me on a promise and as I was building bricks during the day I couldn't wait for finishing time to come and when it did I got back to St Giles rd as quick as I could but stopped off at an off license to get a bottle of Bacardi and a few cans of beer. I suppose it was coming up to 6 pm when I got to my digs, so I had a quick wash and shave and into my room and turned on the radio to a music channel waiting on Matilda to come downstairs, well I waited and waited but no sign of her so I read a book and went to bed at eleven o'clock thinking what's happened ?. I got to work the following day and all the other brickies wanted to know how I got on as I had been keeping them abreast of what was happening, I could have lied but whats the point so I told them the truth and said "ah well that's life".

That night when I finished work I did my usual and went to the pub and had about six or seven pints and back to my digs in St Giles rd, then as I got near to my basement room I could see my bedroom light on and hear music coming from the radio, well I was down the stairs in a shot and opened my bedroom door expecting to see Matilda there but she wasn't anywhere to be seen and the Bacardi bottle was empty, What !!!.

Well I sat on my bed and burst out laughing well what else could I do, I drank the two cans of beer that I had bought with the Bacardi and thought why does it always happen to me, eh. Lol.

When I went to pay Matilda the rent money that Friday night she said to me "she had came into my room earlier that day and thought she'd have a drink of Bacardi to get her in the mood for the music but got carried away", I'd say she got carried away alright she emptied the bloody bottle but the damage had been done so no good crying over spilled milk.[or Bacardi]

Getting back to my job at Colharbour lane there was this guy called Tom who's job it was to keep the two cement mixers filled up as 20 bricklayers used a lot of mortar up during the course of the day, he was a good mixer man but not a very likeable person and too big with his mouth for my liking but I kept out of his way if I could.

He was always being sarcastic to people and in fact a bit of a bully, anyway this night when we had finished work I went into the changing room to change from my working clothes into my

44

good clothes, the changing room was busy with people all trying to get changed and get homeward bound. This Tom who always had cans of beer hidden in the sand beside the mixers had obviously drank a fair bit and he looked over to me and said "you ya Scot's haggis basher why don't you f**k off back to Scotland" Normally I am a quiet person but somethings I will not let go so I strode over to him in two strides and with all my body weight behind my fist hit him on the point of his chin and down he went like a sack of potatoes and as he was laying there I said "you ever talk to me like that again you'll get the same again" and for the rest of my time on the job he kept clear of me, I can't stand bully boys.

I was happy enough working on the barrier block site at £18 per shift then I was offered £19 per shift for a builder called Dave Donnaghue at Peckham hill st which I could walk to through the back doubles in 15 minutes, so I took it as bricklayers are notorious for chopping and changing sites.

It was refurbishment work on a long block of terraced houses with plenty of new garden walls in the back and chimney stacks to get rebuilt and lots of internal alterations, plus all the old brickwork had to be re-pointed, I was happy there so things were looking cool.

While back at my digs one night I heard a terrible scream and rushed out my room to see what was happening, it was Barry he ran past me holding his neck and it looked like his skin was bubbling, it appeared that although Matilda and Barry weren't living as man and wife anymore Matilda had went out to his car to look for something and found a pair of another ladies "undies" on the back seat, when she had came back into the house she'd been frying chips at the time so threw the frying pan with the boiling fat over his head but only hit his neck and I thought oh dear what have I let myself in for here.!!

Then one Friday night when I went to pay Matilda the rent money she came onto me strong [I had a quick look to see there were no chips frying. lol] and she kissed me well I put my arms

45

around her but the next thing I knew was her dog called Peter came out from under the table and bit me on the knee and drew blood. I had to get up to Kings college hospital at Denmark hill and wait for a few hours to get a tetanus jab, bloody hell when was my luck going to change, eh.

On the following night the Saturday I got the number 12 bus down to East st and had a good drink in the Masons and later the Bell, I got into a big company and the drink was going down fast, I couldn't keep up with the pints so I ended up drinking large vodkas and coke. I remember I phoned a mini cab as I could feel myself swaying a bit, cut a long story short the mini cab dropped me outside my digs and I tumbled down the stairs, gets into my room and all of a sudden Matilda is standing there with a glass in her hand and said "this is Nigerian rum punch but its very strong".

The last thing I remember was downing this rum punch in one swallow and then collapsed. I woke up Sunday morning with my head thumping and not a stitch of clothing on !!

Matilda came in and said "you collapsed last night I tried to tell you the rum punch was 140%" bloody hell no wonder I collapsed. She told me she had taken all my clothes off, I said what's the time she said its half past 12 and I though bloody hell the pubs close at 2 in the afternoon on Sundays so I was getting my clothes on when Matilda made it very clear to me that she wanted me to make love to her but I said "I'm not fit for that I'm afraid" and must get a drink to cure my hangover so off I went half running up the road to get to the nearest pub which was the Stirling Castle pub on Camberwell Church st.

I had a couple of Vodkas and a few pints and this calmed me down but I didn't want to go back and face Matilda so I went to the cinema down at Peckham and came out of the cinema at 7 pm just as the pubs were opening and took it easy just drinking a few pints of Lager so I would be OK for work in the morning.

I went to work that week and all was Ok, there was this travelling foreman for Dave Donnaghue [my Guvnor] and his name was Tony Snow from London's East end and he would drive to this site and other sites that Dave had twice a day to see if everything was OK.

On the Thursday of that week myself and the other brickies and hod carriers went to breakfast at our usual time of 10 am, the cafe was about a 7 minutes walk away so we would take about 25 minutes eating our breakfast then and another 7 minute walk back to the site, which worked out about 40 minutes which was about the standard time for breakfast but on this day the cafe owner's assistant never turned up and so it was a slow service.

Cut a long story short it took us just over an hour for break fast and as we were coming back this Tony turned up in his car and looked at his watch and started saying you're all taking the p**s. I tried to explain to him what had happened but he didn't want to know and started shouting and that is when I saw red and said "listen pal don't shout at me, I tried to tell you what happened but you don't want to listen so you can stick your job". "Have all my money ready on Friday" and as it had just turned 11 o'clock I walked over to the Glengall tavern pub right opposite this site and stayed there till closing time at three o'clock.

[Photo of the houses I was working on in Peckham hill st when I told Tony to stick his job]

47

Now what would happen next was unbelievable, after 3 o'clock when the pub closed, I went back over to the site to pick up my tool bag and level and walked back to my digs in St Giles rd and when I arrived there I couldn't believe my eyes the doorway and all the windows of Barry and Matildas house were covered with corrugated sheeting !!! I couldn't get into my digs.

I thought I must be dreaming, I placed my tool bag and level down the at the bottom of the basement stairs and took a walk round the block to clear my head but when I came back it was still the same and just at that moment Barry drove up in his Mercedes car, he came over to me and said "anytime you have a problem come and see me". **What !!!,** well if this wasn't a problem what was?

So I said "I can't get into my room to Barry" and he said its all a big mistake the estate agent/bank or whoever told him he had missed payments on his mortgage and so they had "repossessed" his property and he drove off in his car.

I thought what do I do now, first thing I did was get my club hammer and bolster/chisel from my tool bag and cut the nails on the corrugated sheeting covering the downstairs door pulled back the sheeting, so at least I was in my digs, Aw what a blinking carry on. [I did meet Barry 3 months later and he said "he got his house back again" and when was I going to move back in, I told him next week but never did, do you blame me.?]

So that night I went down to Walworth rd and had a drink in the Rock pub and had a drink with a pal of mine "Andy the butcher" a Cockney mate of mine, he was called this name because he had worked in Dewhursts butchers factory/warehouse on Walworth rd for years and the name had just stuck.

He said "where are you going to live then" and I said "I think I'll get a room over in the Red Lion pub across the road from the Rock". No he said come and stay with me and Evie [his wife] at our place, you can kip on the sofa until you get new digs and I said "thanks very much Andy" and so I went to live at Andy and Evies place on the Doddington estate.

[Photo of the Doddington estate where Andy the butcher and Evie his wife lived]

I went back to the Peckham hill st site to get my wages off of Tony Snow the following day and fair play to him it was all there. Earlier that morning I had been out looking to see if there was any building sites looking for bricklayers and yes a new housing estate called the Salisbury estate was being built in between Chatham st and Flint st, I had talked to the subby called Bill Robb [from Newcastle/Sunderland] and he gave me the start for Monday morning.

I had a drink with Andy the butcher over the weekend in the Rock pub and I slipped him a few quid for putting me up, anyway while drinking in the Rock I got speaking to another Glasgow pal of mine Pat Carney [Paddy] and he said he was living in digs just past Albany rd on Camberwell rd which looked directly over to the tennis courts at Burgess park and he said Danny I'm leaving my digs next week to move in with my daughter and do you want me to put in a good word for you with the landlady for you ? I said "oh yes Pat please"

I have to say that Pat Carney was one of the nicest men I had ever met, an old school Glasgow man and was always good company to have a drink with, his favourite singer was Perry Como and anytime Pat had a drink in him he would break into a Perry Como song. One Saturday night we were having a drink in the Surrey Gardens arms pub and it was near to closing time and we were all hanging onto our almost empty pint glasses [hoping for afters] when Pat who was wearing a cardigan [with pockets in it] accidentally dropped the cigarette he was smoking into one of his cardigan pockets and it started to smoulder. Andy the Butcher picked up our almost empty pint glasses from the table we were standing beside and threw them over Pat's burning pocket, it did the trick but we had nothing left in our pint glasses and at that moment the barmaid passing by us picked our glasses up placing them on her tray and we had to leave the pub then. No afters for us that night and no Perry Como songs either. !!!

Sadly Pat Carney passed away after a very short illness, Pat was one of the good guys of our World, he'd come to London as a young man with his best mate Jimmy McGinley, who was also a terrific person. God Bless and watch over the two of them.

- - - - -

Chapter 4

The Salisbury Estate

Come the Monday morning and I start work on the Salisbury estate and start working with a bricklayer from Walworth called Johnny Donovan whom I would later work with for a good few years. John lived down Wansey st where Walworth Town hall stands although he told me he previously had lived in Penrose house at Penrose street just behind Carter st police station with his wife Flo, Son Stephen and daughter Susan. About 14 bricklayers were working here and the pay was £18 per day [minus tax] anyway the first couple of hours the subby or foreman bricklayer would keep their eye on you to see if you were a good brickie or not and after the first day the subby had me building all the face brick corners, see if your corners were built correctly then your wall would be good if the corner was built wrong then your wall would be wrong.

[Photo of the Salisbury estate taken from Chatham st, which at the time of the Salisbury being built, were being refurbed by builder Patsy Pattton who I would work for a few times. I will mention Chatham st later in my book and you won't believe what happened !!]

I settled in there pretty quickly and they seemed a nice bunch of lads except this one bricklayer called John Greig [also the name of the Glasgow Rangers football captain who was a great player for club and country]. As it happened he was a Rangers football fan too and me being a Glasgow Celtic fan we had different views but I always say every one is entitled to their views. The ironic thing is I have pals who are Rangers supporters and we can share a bit or banter no prob but not this geezer.

Some of the bricklayers like me were self employed while some worked direct on their cards and as we had bank holidays coming up the brickies working on the cards got paid but the self employed didn't although Bill Robb paid me for the bank holidays as I was a good bricklayer and could build all the fancy brickwork.

Oh by the way my pal Pat Carney had left his digs at Albany rd/Camberwell rd and he told me to go and see the Landlady Mrs Ullman [who was Hungarian]. I went to see Mrs Ullman and she said "I hope you are not like Mr Carney who came home drunk and was always losing his keys". !!!. I said "Mrs Ullman I do like a drink but don't get drunk [only sometimes ha ha] and I don't lose keys", so she said OK you can move in at £12 per week and once again my digs were at the very top of the house.

So I had been on the building of the Salisbury estate [where I would actually live later with my wife] for a few months and all was good it was a happy site and lots of brickies like myself like to sing while we work as it causes a good atmosphere but that other bricklayer John Greig kept sniping at me and tried to bring me into arguement's about Celtic v Rangers but I wouldn't bite.

Then one morning we were all queing up in the site canteen for breakfast when this John Greig started horse-play with me and put his arm round my neck and started to choke me, so I dug my elbow into his ribs, he let go and then we stood toe to toe trading punches, in the background I could hear the canteen lady's screaming then all the other brickies and hoddies jumped in and separated us.

Bill the guvnor came to me after breakfast time and said "I know that John is an A******e but he has worked with me for years" and I said "well Bill its not going to end here, **you know that don't you**, the two of us will be at it again given the first "wrong look" so he came back later and said to me I will transfer him to another site of mine over in North London and I said fair enough Bill and perhaps just as well.

I bought the canteen lady's a box of chocolates each and apologized for upsetting them. It never ceases to amaze me that no matter what site I have ever worked on that there is always some idiot to cause bad feeling, while all the time the majority of people just want to get on with each other.

So by this time I had moved into Mrs Ullman's digs and would take a leisurely stroll at night time after work, might have a sandwich and cuppa in one of the cafes on Walworth rd and then have a pint down the Lane or in the Kings head then walk up to the Rock pub where I was using as my headquarters as it was the pub nearest to me [with the exception of the Fountain pub but I hardly ever used there.] Then one morning I woke up in my digs had a wash and shave and walked down Walworth rd to get to my work and I couldn't believe it the newspaper billboards had "the King is dead" and "Elvis dies", I couldn't believe it as Elvis was my favourite singer.

I went to work in a very bad mood that morning and it seemed that everybody I talked to couldn't believe the news either, I think it was a Tuesday [for us] when Elvis died, there wasn't any singing from me that day I can tell you. When I finished work at 5 pm that night it was an eerie feeling and later when the Pubs opened at 5.30 it seemed every pub I passed was playing Elvis records and it was like that for the rest of the week.

Now a funny thing happened to me which I will explain, I finished up work on a Thursday night and went to Mary's cafe on Walworth rd just before Albany rd, she was a Turkish girl and she and her husband Hassan ran a great cafe with great food but they were always shouting at each other [must have been true love, eh.]

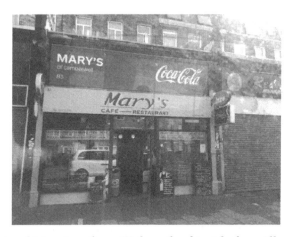

[Photo of Mary's cafe on Walworth rd just before Albany rd]

So I walks up to my digs at Mrs Ullmans and puts my hand in my pocket for the keys but nothing, no keys !!!! I quickly went back into Mary's and said "have I dropped my keys, they looked but no keys".

I quickly went back down to the Salisbury estate and Mick the site agent was just on his way home and about to lock the site gates up when I said "Mick quick let me in I must have dropped my house keys here" and fair play to Mick he came and helped me look for them. Unfortunately no keys.

I walked back to my digs with a heavy heart I can tell you and had to face the inevitable, so I knocked on Mrs Ullmans door and a lady friend of hers opened the door and I said "I live here but have lost my house keys". She said come in and it so happened Mrs Ullman was having a tea party with her fellow Hungarian lady friends and I stood there telling her I had lost my keys. She went ballistic saying you are just like Mr Carney, I will now have to get these special keys cut at great expense.

I said "I will pay for them Mrs Ullman and she said **of course you will pay for them**" !!, standing in front of all those ladies I felt my face turn crimson red and wished the floor would have opened up and swallowed me, she begrudgingly held me a new seat of keys, they were only small slim keys so I thought I'll get a larger key ring to put them on and hopefully won't lose them again.

Right, away I went upstairs and went to my room and thought I'll go downstairs to the bathroom and have a bath. I was taking my clothes off and when I took my shoes off I couldn't believe it, there were my missing keys !!.

Somehow when I had been changing from my work clothes to my going home clothes these slim keys with only a piece of wire holding them together had slipped down in between the outside of my sock and the inside of my shoe.

I had my bath and got dressed ready to go out and celebrate, I ran down the stairs and knocked on Mrs Ullmans door to tell her the good news saying here are your other keys back its alright.

She said "its not alright I'm giving you a weeks notice you will leave your room next Friday". What ??, but there was no good arguing the point, so instead of going to the Rock pub to celebrate it was down to the Rock to drown my sorrows but like all set backs in my life I just dusted myself down and said ah

Well Danny boy, as one door closes another door opens and no good crying over spilled milk.[or lost keys]

[Photo of my digs at Mrs Ullmans, 1ˢᵗ door left was my door, top floor window was mine]

I thought I must get new digs again so that week working on the Salisbury estate I thought I will try and get digs just off East st, but sitting in the pub one night after finishing work I bought the evening standard newspaper and on the work section they were advertising for bricklayers over in West Germany again and I thought right Danny boy why not. So I told Bill Robb my guvnor on the Salisbury that I was heading off to West Germany at the weekend and he said "I'm sorry to see you go son but listen remember if it don't work out you'll always have a job here as you're a good brickie".

So off to W. Germany at the weekend and once again its "Foxy" me and the other bricklayers who meet at Charing cross railway station and soon were in Holland and at Nijmegen to be transported to various building sites throughout West Germany [just like the TV show Aufwiedersehen Pet] but as I say I wont discuss this here but in Part 2 of my book.

landing back in London after been away for 6 months working in West Germany I end up living in a room in the Red Lion pub on Walworth rd. I'm now working only a short distance away in Grosvenor terrace for Dave Donnaghue again doing loads of refurbishment work, building garden walls, Chimney stacks and loads of re-pointing the brickwork. I was using the Rock pub again and have a story to tell you about that.

The Rock music lounge was very well known in Walworth for great singers and the really good new was that at weekend nights the music lounge stayed open until one am, if you had been drinking in another pub you could get in after eleven o'clock [normal pub closing time back then] but you had to pay £1 on the door to get in but it was well worth it.

There used to be one guy in the Rock who would get up and sing a song while bashing a tin tray off his head, it was hilarious. Of course some times there was a punch-up there which put a damper on things but usually as soon as the fight started it was over and everybody got back to drinking and enjoying the music and singing.

[Photo of the Rock bar on Walworth rd]

Charlie and Sylvie ran the pub with their son young Charlie and it was a great pub and most people got on with each other. Everybody knew each other and there was always a card school being played in the public bar or people playing a game of pool, in fact I think the Rock was one of the first pubs in Walworth to have this new pool game installed in the early 70s. There was one guy called "Gabby John" and boy could he "rabbit", no harm in the man put a non stop "Yapper". When people saw him come in the pub they lowered their heads so they wouldn't see him. Anyway the good thing is he only came in the pub once a week either a Friday night or a Saturday lunch time, one Saturday lunch time he came in, ordered a pint from Charlie [senior] and then said "oh dear I've left my flat without my wallet, lend me a couple of quid Charlie and I'll pay you back next time I'm in". So Charlie gave him a sub of a couple of pounds and all was well.

The following week on a Thursday night I was running short and pay day was tomorrow so I said to Charlie [senior] "can I borrow a few quid off of you till tomorrow Charlie" and he said "no !!, he said I'm not saying you wouldn't pay me back but I don't loan out money and I felt like saying but you gave Gabby a sub but I never, I just said OK".

So the following night I walked into the Rock and Charlie [senior] served me, I ordered a pint and said to Sylvie and Young Charlie behind the bar "would you like a drink and they said yes please", I said "I wont offer to buy you a drink Charlie because you refuse to loan me a couple of quid last night" and Charlie got embarrassed which was good because he knew what I had felt like last night. In fact I did this a couple of times, until Sylvie came over to me one night when I was sitting down and she said "Charlie shouldn't have refused you as you're a good customer Danny, anytime you want a sub during the week come and see me".

While working on Grosvenor terrace there were lots of other trades working there and there were 6 painters who had John Sullivan as their foreman or "Sully" as everyone called him, at night time when I finished work I would go to the Rock for a drink and so did these painters. Sully would come in with a few of his painters and he would say "because I'm the foreman I don't need to buy a drink" and I thought "Jackass".

Anyway I would usually be drinking with a few mates like John McQuade and his wife Carol or Pat Carney, etc . One Saturday night I was all suited and booted and went to the sit down cubicle in the Rock bar toilet and when I came out went to wash my hands when Sully who was standing beside me at the wash hand basin said your braces are hanging down, I looked and sure enough I hadn't buttoned up my braces so I said" thanks John".

The following week after work I was having a drink in the Rock and it was about 9 pm and Sully's painters had left just leaving him [to buy his own drink], I was at the bar buying a pint from Young Charlie when Sully came up to me and said "buy me a pint otherwise I will tell people about your braces hanging down". **What!!!** I said "what kind of stupid statement is that, I said no I wont buy you a pint in fact the only thing you will get from me is a punch on the jaw". Young Charlie said "John you're out of order go away and sit down" of which he did. I had a few more beers after that then crossed the road to the Red Lion pub where I had a room just as I was walking in the door I saw Sully come flying out of the Rock public bar door and he saw me but pretended to be looking up and down Walworth rd for me.

I could just imagine him walking back into the Rock and saying I was going to sort him out but I can't see him, anyway the following night after work I'm in the Rock bar just putting money into the pool table and Sully walks in and marches over to me and says "You were out of order last night" and I said "No I wasn't out of order but you were, but listen cut the crap there are two ways we can sort this out, one we can walk outside and settle this with our fists or we can shake hands and forget it. I personally would rather shake hands and forget it but the choice is up to you".

Of course the whole pub had went deathly quiet [you could have heard a pin drop]. Anyway Sully says "no I would rather shake hands" of which we did and no I never did buy him a pint. !!Just across from the Rock on the other side of the road but down a bit was the Fountain pub, a new Guvnor took it over and wanted it painted inside and outside so he got Sully to do it because fair play to him he was a good painter. When Sully walked it was a kind of shuffle he did, but anyway he done a first class job and the Guvnor took such a shine to him that he changed the name of the pub from the Fountain to "Sully Shuffles" what a great achievement in life to have a pub named after you, eh.

By this time I had heard that my old Guvnor Dave Sullivan was building flats on Waterloo rd just past St George's circus, so I phoned him up and he said "yes start on there when ever you want".

I told Dave Donnaghue who I was working for on Grosvenor terrace that I would be leaving him on Friday and he said he didn't want to lose me but I said I just fancy a change and he said "come back anytime Danny".

So I starts on the Waterloo job on Monday morning and the foreman bricklayer was called John Ederidge from the East end of London and I got on with him very well.

[Photo above is of the Flats on Waterloo rd we built for Dave Sullivan.]

It was another Laing's site and there were about 18 bricklayers there and about 8 hod carriers, again it was a happy site with the brickies and a few hoddies singing or cracking jokes but still working hard. Roy Motram the bricklayer who I worked mates with on the building of the Heygate was now Dave Sullivan's business partner and would be popping down to this Job and Dave's other jobs more or less like a contracts manager and would bring out our wages on a Friday [or maybe a Thursday as it was a week in hand for the money now].

All the guys on the site nicknamed Roy "Red neck" because his face was always flushed/red and we had a canteen lady called Babs who ran the canteen on our site, she was a lovely girl and Roy and her started "living in sin" together. In fact one day I walked into the canteen unexpected and Babs was trying to kiss Roy and he said "Oh Babs no, not in front of Danny" ha ha.

Babs had a son called Gary and he was one of the hod carriers on our site and a nice lad and he was nicknamed by us as "Son of red neck" which Gary hated saying "He's not my f*****g Dad".

One of the hod carriers on the job was called Billy and he lived in a hostel nicknamed "The White-house", it was at number 112 st Georges rd almost opposite the Prince of Wales pub on st George's rd just down from the Elephant and Castle roundabout it was called the White-house because it was painted all in white.

Actually an Irish couple from County Cork had bought this property just before World war 2 started [they bought one section of it first and later when they had the money bought the rest of it]. It was a huge place and had about 80 - 90 working men living there. Some 10 to a room all single beds, other rooms slept 3 and other rooms 2 people. Rooms cleaned and bed sheets changed once a week, a television down in the lounge where you ate your meals, it was great.

*[Photo above is of the entrance to the White-house
at 112 st Georges rd down from Elephant]*

Mr and Mrs Wall gave you a breakfast in the morning and an evening meal, all brought to your table [waiter service]. You had breakfast, Lunch and an evening salad on Sundays. Many men used this as a springboard before getting married and having families and some came back to visit Mr and Mrs Wall, he could be a bit grumpy but Mrs Wall was old school and everyone loved her.

I wonder how many people passed by this building on the bus going to work and never knew the history behind it, anyway Billy said to me "why don't you leave the Red Lion pub and move into the White-house" which I did and loved it [but not at first.]

I moved in on a Friday night, it was also ran by Mr and Mrs Walls sons so it was all a family affair. I saw Peter Wall one of the sons and paid my rent and he put me in a room with two other guys, we all had a single bed and not much room but then again after a hard days work and a few beers you just wanted to get your head down. Every morning at 5 am one of the other guys had an alarm clock that went off at that time and as soon as it did he sat bolt upright and started polishing /dubbin his boots, then go back to sleep and at 6 am another alarm clock would go off and he sat bolt upright and started polishing his boots again. I thought to myself oh dear what have I let myself in for here.The other guy could hear this too.

The White-house was only a five minute walk away so it was nice and handy for me and I enjoyed working on this Waterloo rd job. Now then I was walking up Walworth rd one Saturday afternoon heading towards the Good Intent pub when I bumped into Johnny Donovan who I had worked with on the Salisbury estate and I said "why don't you start on my job as Dave Sullivan is paying £20 per shift" and John was still getting £18 with Bill Robb on the Salisbury so he said "yes I will". Fair play to John he did start [I had OK'd it with John the foreman bricklayer on my site].

So me and John were working together as mates building walls and John was a good bricklayer too and a nice lad to work with. We worked till 1.30 Saturday afternoon and got paid the full shift on this site but I had told John the foreman bricklayer I would only work till 12 noon and had already told this to Dave Sullivan and all I got paid was half a shift but that was fine by me as it let me get to the pub at 12 instead of 1.30 [remember it was 3 in the afternoon closing time back then]. The nearest pub to us was the Tower bar on Tower bridge rd only a few minutes walk from out site and it was here that I met Mo [Maureen] the barmaid whom I would later marry although we never went out for ages, I asked her out a few time but I think she was playing hard to get lol.

So getting back to the Whitehouse I had been there for two weeks and this guy's alarm clock was still going off at 5 and 6 in the morning and him sitting bolt upright and polishing his boots. One Friday night the other guy in our room who was a big giant of a man from Galway in the west of Ireland came in after the pub had closed and walked over to this guys bed, unzipped his trouser zip and p****d all over the boot polisher. Well your man let out a roar and started screaming, Peter Wall the owners son who lived on the premises came rushing in and tried to sort out all the mayhem. He asked me what had happened and I told him the full story, he said to me "you should have told me about the alarm clock carry on" and I said "but I'm not a grass Peter". The upshot was the two other guys got the red card and were turfed out and I was transferred to a smaller room where there were only two single beds with a quiet guy in there called Keith.

I would use the Albert arms which was just round the corner from the White-house in Garden row/ Gladstone st and officially known as the Elephant area, at that time an Irish landlord called Eugene ran it, he had a few customers in there who were on "The book" or as some say on "The slate" he would have a little book and tear one of the pages out and mark your name down and the price of each drink you bought and come payday you paid him back. I was shocked when some of these guys who were on "the slate" got an "extra" drink added against their name when they were in the toilet so I thought right Danny boy don't go "on the slate" in this pub. What a terrible thing to do,eh. !!!

Most nights when I finished work I would have my evening meal in the Whitehouse and go to the Albert arms or take a walk to the Elephant having a drink in the Prince of Wales or Gibralter on St Georges rd or maybe the Pineapple or the Charlie Chaplin pubs. We were actually spoiled for choices as there were so many pubs round the Elephant at that time although with the regeneration programme lots had disappeared and sadly lots more would disappear in years to come. Every time I was at the Elephant I always looked over at Perronet house and remembered fondly that this was my first building site in South London.

Back to our site at Waterloo rd and John Ederidge the foreman bricklayer was cutting a bit of dampcourse with a Stanley knife and he was kneeling down on the ground to do it and he accidentally pulled the Stanley knife back too quickly and it ripped into his leg and there was blood everywhere. As luck would have it the St John's Ambulance station was almost next door so an Ambulance was quick on site and took John away to hospital, he would be off of work for 4 weeks and fair play to Dave Sullivan he paid him full wages while off.

Dave then asked me would I be foreman bricklayer until John came back and I said "no problem". I ran the job and it was alright, all the other brickies and hoddies respected me and I in turn respected them. Although I never got on with the site agent called George Edwards who thought he was a cut above everyone else, he came down to the canteen at breakfast time one morning and said to me in front of everybody "right you have all had long enough for your tea-break". I said to him "listen pal I don't work for you, only Dave Sullivan can tell me what to do" and with that I said to all the other brickies and hoddies "right lads go up and order another cuppa for yourselves from Babs".

Of course everyone was watching to see what happened and he said right I will phone up Dave and I said it wont change things. Anyway I spoke to Dave on the phone and said "I'm running the job and wont have my authority undermined if you don't agree then get yourself another foreman" but Dave said "no probs Danny carry on regardless", then John the foreman came back and it was good to see him because he was an OK guy and I handed back the foreman-ship to him.

There was one thing I used to hate in the building trade and that was wet days, you would get on site and be sitting in the canteen and it would be lashing down with rain [and bricklayers cant build bricks in wet weather]. I got on the Waterloo rd site and one morning it was bucketing down so we sat around playing cards and to be truthful if I don't start work first thing in the morning I lose interest, it was still lashing down at 10.30 am and John Donovan and me had made our minds up we were going to the Tower pub at 11 o'clock opening time. At five to eleven it was only just the odd drop of rain and Roy Motram came on site and said to everyone what do you want to do work or pub, Me and John said Pub !! but everyone else went to work which is fair enough, a person has to do what they think best, so me and John headed off to the Tower for a game of pool and a rake of beer and me chatting to Mo.!!!

Babs the canteen girl was having a terrible row with Roy one morning, it appeared that they had split up and all the jewellery that Roy had bought her while they were together had taken back and she was calling him all the names under the sun. Ah well I know partnerships break down but I think that was mean what Roy did to Babs.

So this site at Waterloo was nearing completion of the brickwork, Dave still had the big job at Blackfriars still going so he transferred my self and John Donovan there and all went well there, there was lots of brickwork there and was only a short bus journey for me to get there. Then another bricklayer I knew Damian Flanagan said "would you like to move into a flat in Oswin st just at the Elephant". He said he knew the landlady very well and she had a spare large room to let and would I be interested . So I went to have a look at the place and it was magic it had a large bedroom with a double bed and a large open front room which would be my front room and kitchen/diner and a large front window which opened fully outwards I took it immediately and yes it was at the very top of the house again. Lol

[Photo of my top floor flat in Oswin st, 2nd bay window from the left, my flat at the very top.]

I told Peter Wall in the Whitehouse I was leaving and he said "anytime you want a place back here its no problem Danny" [I would be back there a few times in the future]. Anyway the swimming baths had been built at the Elephant and the leisure centre/squash courts were being built so I left Dave Sullivan as this site was just a couple of minutes walk from my flat in Oswin st. I have to say that this site was in disarray there were about 12 bricklayers there and there had never been a foreman bricklayer there. No levels had been put round the job for the brickies to work off of. Anyway I had been there about two weeks and Peter Pritchard who was from County Cavan in Ireland and a good friend of mine was a kind of supervisor there but Peter never had a knowledge of brickwork so he asked me would I become foreman bricklayer.

I said "its a bit late in the day to be getting a foreman" but because he was a friend of Mine I said yes.I got the site engineer to shoot me a few datum levels round the brickwork so everyone knew what finished height we would be working too and after a week the job was in much better shape although there was probably only about 6 weeks brickwork left there. Techno was the main contractor, they were a Yorkshire firm and they paid a weekly check to a guy called Michael Gaughan who in turn would pay all of us [in cash].

[Photo of swimming baths left hand side and squash courts to the right hand side]

Peter Pritchard always drove to this Mick Gaughan's office/house to get the wages and was back on site about 5 pm and paid everyone out. Actually this is where I met Kevin McNicholas [who later be the Guvnor of the Beehive pub in Penrose st] he wasn't much cop as a bricklayer and Gaughan said to me sack him !!!.

Then Kevin came to me almost crying and said "oh please don't sack me Danny I need the money", so I told Gaughan I needed a brickie to cut holes in the brickwork to allow the plumber to get his pipes through, so I agreed with Gaughan to keep Kevin on.

This Friday night it was an hour after finishing time and no Peter and no wages, I had money on me so took the lads to the Two Eagles pub just along a bit on Brook drive [opposite the hospital] and bought everyone a drink and an hour later Peter turned up with the wages but I was smelling a rat !!! I wish I would have followed my instincts and "jacked" this site in because the same thing happened next week and we never got paid at all. Everyone got knocked for their wages, what a terrible feeling to have worked hard all week and not get paid. I'm afraid the building trade was infamous for people getting"knocked" for their wages but there's not much you can do.

We contacted this Gaughan guy and he said the firm "Techno" hadn't paid him so he couldn't pay us, we confronted the site agent and he said the firm had paid Gaughan the money, cut a long story short everybody was gutted then the site agent said to me and the other bricklayers "you can start working with "Techno" direct on Monday and your wages will be safe" [would they ??] the agent said to me "will you stay on as foreman bricklayer" and I said "you must be bloody joking" and I left but some of the other bricklayers decided to stay and I suppose that that was in the forlorn hope they would get the wages they had been "knocked" for but I don't think they ever did. So there's a bit of Elephant history for you folks.

So I was loving my living at Oswin st and had started back work with Dave Sullivan but out at Grove Park it was a housing estate and there was lots of work there, John Ederidge [from Waterloo job] was once again the foreman bricklayer and my old mate Johnny Donovan from Wansey st. was there too. Dave had a van that picked us up at the Elephant in the morning so it was about a twenty five minute drive to the site and all was well. I had started to go out with Mo by this time and we would have a drink or go to the cinema at the Elephant at the weekend and go back to Mo's place at Aldbridge st which was just off the Old Kent rd.

This is when I also met Tracy my eldest girl, I know I'm not Tracy's biological father but she is my daughter the same as Susan and Danielle is, no difference at all. Mo's Mum Eileen would baby sit Tracy while we were out. I had already met Mo's Dad Alfie as he was the barman in the Tower bar where Mo also worked and he was a great character who I liked very much. [I have a few stories to tell about the Tower pub later]

Mo had the bottom floor of her Mum and dad's house and like lots of the houses back then it had a warm homely feeling about it, of course one draw back was the toilet was outside in the back garden/yard but that's just the way life was back then and no shame in it.

Anyway Mo and me had being going out for a good while, then and Mo was offered a brand new council house on the new Salisbury estate, yes the one that I had been on the building of. Mo took it and I went with her to measure up curtains, carpets etc and Mo asked me "to move in with her" and I said "yes".

So goodbye to my landlady Emma at Oswin st and moved into number 3 Salisbury close with Mo and we were now officially "living in sin". It was a nice place with central heating and two bedrooms with a wee park down off Chatham st where the kids could play and then we found out Mo was expecting, so we decided to get married.

We went to Walworth town hall and done all the paperwork and the wedding date was for January 5th 1979, I was 30 years old and would be 31 on January the 11th. My parents came down from Glasgow as did my sister and brother in law. It was a Friday we got married and I went to work until 12 noon as we got married in Walworth town hall at 4 in the afternoon.

I have to say though as it was January time the weather was cold and it was a bad winter that year, so we couldn't build bricks until the temperature was 34 F and rising otherwise the brickwork built would never "knit together" and a week later you could kick it over as it had never set. So we would sit in the site canteen till about 11 am till the temperature was OK and then we built bricks, but about 2.30 pm the temperature was falling down and we had to stop work. [But we had to cover up all the work we had built] This meant we were only working about three and half hours per day and less than half a weeks wages. !!! So it was quite common to have a sub to bolster your wakes on a Friday and I was in there like a shot.

[Photo of Walworth Town hall. Where Mo and me married on January 5th 1978]

To be truthful I was really skint and said to Dave I'm getting married can you loan me some money and he gave me a "personal loan" of £100 which would be deducted each week off my wages. Thank God for that as I hadn't even bought Mo a wedding ring and that Friday when I finished work at 12 noon I got down to the Elephant castle shopping centre and bought Mo a wedding ring for about £40 and the alcohol for our wedding reception which we held at our flat in Salisbury close and then quickly back to our flat to change into the suit I would get married in.

I thought I wish I had saved money up, but knowing what I was like I knew I was always a spender and not a saver, I am, what I am, I am.

- - - - -

Chapter 5

Married Life

So that was me married which I never thought I would be but I suppose a lot of us never thought we would get married, eh. I was still working out at Grove park for Dave Sullivan a strange thing happened, John Ederidge the foreman bricklayer "blotted his copy book" he had told Dave he was ill and he hadn't came into work for two weeks but it was found out that he had been working and working only a short distance from Dave's office which was on the Aylesbury estate and to rub salt into the wounds he had been given a firms car by Dave and was driving it from the East end of London to the job he was working on which was only on Flint st Walworth just in front of Tisdall place/Flint st where he was building new houses.

He was "grassed up" by a hod carrier of Dave's but I wont mention his name but when Dave heard, him and Roy Motram went on site to face him and Dave said "I've been good to you, I paid you full wages when you cut your leg when I didn't have to because you're self employed" John said "I felt like a break" and Dave said "well you should have told me and you could have left for a while but then came back, you've went behind my back and that I cannot forgive, so give me the car keys back". John held the car keys over and I never saw him again which was a pity as he not only was a good bricklayer but a good foreman.

This was a great big site at Grove park and Dave had about 20 brickies and 10 hoddies working there but the Clerk of Works was one horrible person who I had already had a few run ins with. This Clerk of works was so full of his own importance and loud mouthed, he would go over to bricklayers building a wall and say I don't like this or I don't like that and I had already told him he was out of order speaking to the men.

I said " I realise you have a job to do but if you have any complaints to make then its done by chain of command, which means you either tell the sub contractor or his foreman who then in turn will pass on the message to the men working underneath them". I also said "you are a bully trying to intimidate men so do yourself a favour and never speak to me like that you tosspot" this didn't go down to well with him especially when John the foreman had agreed with me in front of the Clerk of works [this is before John blotted his copybook].

This incensed this Clerk of works who went on to knit pick on every bit of brickwork built on the site, cut a long story short Dave ended up losing £70.000 on this job when it finished a year later. Laing the main contractor covered him for £40.000 of it. Before this happened I had taken ill in February [about 6 weeks after being married] it had been a cold winter and I was going into my flat in the Salisbury estate which had the central heating on full blast that I contracted Bronchial pneumonia. One night after work I could hardly breathe and somehow managed to get myself round to my Doctor in East st who was Dr Wetherup. [opposite the Masons arms pub]

He happened to leave his room to get something from his receptionist and after taking one look at me said "come into my room immediately", he checked me over and he said "you have pneumonia lad". He stopped his surgery there and then and drove me home in his car saying to my wife "prop him up in bed with pillows behind him so the phlegm doesn't lay on his lungs and turn this heating down and keep the window open to let fresh air in. I'll be back in the morning to check on him" and when he did, I heard him say to Mo "I don't like the colour of his skin, I had turned an ashen-grey colour by all accounts and he called for an ambulance. The ambulance men came to take me away and I was semi delirious by this time, I thought it was the police and was struggling and trying to fight against them.

73

Cut a long story short my Doctor had been giving me penicillin which he found out later I was allergic to, I was in hospital at Guys at London bridge and I was very poorly, in fact I was told later that they had given me two days to live if they didn't hit on the right combination of medication but fortunately I did make a full recovery but I lost a lot of weight and was very weak. Two days before I was sent home the head surgeon had come round my bedside with about ten students with him and he said "well Mr Gill you had us all worried there for a while but you are recovered now" he told all his students what had happened to me as this was all part of their learning.

He made me lean over in bed and put a few of his fingers over the back of my lungs and tapped them with his other fingers while asking me to say out aloud "99" to get an echo of how good/bad my lungs were. He seemed satisfied and then got the other ten students to to do the exact same thing to me and each time they drummed their fingers over my lungs I had to say "99" and when the last student said to me say "99" I said oh for F***'s sake "100" and they all burst out laughing. The Surgeon said any questions for us Mr Gill and I said yes I have one, my wife brought me up a tin of Guinness yesterday but the ring pull is broken and I can't get it open, he said to one of the students hand Mr Gill a steel punch and I drove it into the top of the Guinness tin and it opened it up ok but unfortunately sprayed all the students. They all walked away with the Surgeon saying yes Mr Gill you are definitely on the road to recovery.

The following day just before I went home a young lady physiotherapist said can I do my exam-test on you please and I said of course and she lifted up my pyjama top and was massaging my back to get any remaining phlegm off my lungs/chest and just at that moment my wife came onto the ward shouting out you dirty swine what do you think you're doing. I said Mo the young lady is doing an exam of me, Mo said I'll make an example of you when we get out of here. Bloody hell a man can't win,eh. Mind you the physiotherapist was gorgeous looking.

So we got a mini cab back to the Salisbury estate and we ended up in bed for a kiss and a cuddle [oh la la] and then at three o'clock went to pick Tracy up from school but the walking had left me a bit weak and perhaps the kissing and cuddling too ha ha. I went the next day to Dr Wetherup's surgery in East st and I was told by the receptionist "Mr Gill go straight in" [jumping the queue] well Dr Wetherup was out of his chair in a shot and shook me by the hand vigorously saying "you were playing a dangerous game there laddie", actually I think he was glad that I hadn't "kicked the bucket" as he had been giving me penicillin which I was allergic to [he should have checked this out] but I never held a grudge against him for that. I never saw Dr Wetherup again until I wanted a vasectomy a few years later.

I phoned up Dave Sullivan and told him I can work again and he said right Danny I'm putting you and Johnny Donovan to work on the Aylesbury estate.

[Photo of the Aylesbury estate under construction on Wendover block at Thurlow st]

So John and me start work on the Aylesbury in 1979, remember the Aylesbury had been built between 1963-1977, we had to do remedial work on some of the boundary/garden walls that had been damaged by vandals. We reported on the Monday morning to the Clerk of works who was called Ted Bell and he was a nice guy, he said "we have lots of brick walls damaged" by vandals so we repair them to their former state. We had a hod carrier called John Kay who lived in the red brick buildings in the middle of the Aylesbury estate. There was a works-compound on the ground floor of the Wendover block that had the cement mixer in it and all the bricks we required and loads of other stuff and yes the dumper truck was kept in there too. No materials could be left out overnight because all these "Little Herberts" would throw bricks through windows etc.

We had to sign in on the site book every morning but got John or hoddie to sign in the three of us every morning and at the same time in the morning sign us out for the five o'clock finish. Ted the Clerk of works showed us a sketch where all the walls we were to repair were situated as this Aylesbury estate was massive. First thing then on Monday morning John our hoddie put a mix of mortar in the cement mixer drove it down to the first wall and then went back in the dumper truck to get the bricks from the compound and bring them to us. Our first job was chisel away the hardened mortar where the bricks had been and then start afresh building the wall back up to its original height.

Johnny Donovan and me got a shock because as we were building the bricks somebody started taking pot shots at us from an air rifle, I could hear the "whizz" of the air slugs passing by my ear and then "ping" as they hit the ground. Bloody hell what have we let ourselves in for here I said to Johnny. We went for shelter and waited over an hour and went back to building up the wall and thank God no more air rifles shooting at us. We had a site canteen above the work-compound place and also Ted Bells office was there, he was the main man on the site and he dealt with all money matters, there were glaziers working there daily repairing broken windows it was a constant year to year job for them.

There were also carpenters, plumbers, tilers and asphalters carrying out remedial daily works, The Aylesbury was allocated a given amount of money each year, once that limit had been reached then only the really necessary work was covered. The next day we went to work we looked at the walls we had repaired yesterday and they had been knocked down again, we went to see Ted Bell and he said this is the kind of site that you keep building the walls back up again until one morning you come in and its still standing. It was annoying but that is just the way it was and at the end of the day we were paid our wages whether the walls stayed up or had to be rebuilt again but what a waste of public money. !!!

We always had our breakfast in the site canteen ran by a lady called Joyce who lived in Albridge st [yes same street as my wife Mo came from and she knew her.] and Ted Bell as I said had his office nearby, so he knew where to contact us with any new orders, this saved him walking halfway round the estate to find us. One morning at breakfast time Ted said to us "I have a big wall for you to build beside the Bricklayers arms in Westmoreland rd"

[Photo of the Bricklayers arms with the wall
we built to the right hand side]

77

We started building it on a Wednesday, John or hoddie would bring the bricks down from the compound in the dumper and we would stack them on the pavement, then John went back to the compound and put a couple of mixes of mortar into the cement mixer and brought that down in the dumper and Johnny and me started building this 6 feet high wall but it was pretty long and would keep us going for a week.

We were asked by Ted Bell to come in Saturday and continue building it, so we said OK, we would work till one o'clock and get paid the shift for it. Come Saturday it was a bit of a disaster, Johnny Donovan and me started taking down all the spare bricks left over from yesterday from the top of the wall and stacked them on the pavement while our hoddie went to put a mortar mix in the cement mixer and bring it down in the dumper truck. Half an hour later John came walking back down to us and said "the dumper has a flat tyre" so we were knackered. Ted Bell wasn't on site as he never worked Saturday's, so all the bricks we had taken off the top of the wall and put on the pavement was in vain and had to put them back on the top of the wall again and brush the pavement clear and we were in the cafe in Arnside st at 9 o'clock having breakfast.

I went home and told Mo what had happened, she was taking Tracy round to her Mum and Dads [who had moved from Aldbridge st to Sharstead st at the Kennington end of Walworth] Mo was almost due to give birth so I walked them round and then went for a drink in the Faunce pub just nearby for a couple of hours and then walked them home to our flat in Salisbury close. Come Monday morning and Roy Motram turned up and wanted to know why we never worked Saturday, we told him it wasn't our fault the dumper had a flat tyre and he said OK and agreed to pay us half a shift, so that wasn't bad. Then a old lady came out of her house and went up to Roy and said "are you the Guvnor" Roy said "yes" well the lady ripped into Roy saying "I've never seen anything like it in my life, your men come at 8 am and take the bricks off the wall and then put them back on top of the wall and go home" Roy was getting redder in the face trying to explain to the lady but she didn't want to know, I know it must have looked stupid but there you are these things happen.

So the fitter was called out to sort out the flat tyre on the dumper first thing Monday morning and we were building bricks again by ten thirty am and finished the wall on Wednesday night, of course we had a few drinks in the Bricklayers arms when were building the wall Ann was the barmaids name and it was a lovely pub. I had used it in the past and it was one of the few remaining pubs to have a shove halfpenny table and had mid week matches with other pubs. It had a nice homely feeling to the pub and the Guvnor and his wife always made you welcome as did all the pubs in Walworth may I add.

Mo's water broke and her Mum sensing it was near the time was in our house to look after our Tracy, we got an ambulance and went to Guys hospital where Susan was born at 6 o'clock on Thursday morning weighing 7lb 3 oz's. I was with Mo all the way through the birth and the nurses/midwifes were making me cups of tea and asking what songs would I like to hear while Mo was shouting out "Epidural, I want more epidural" It was a moving experience for me and I was glad I experienced it. While Mo was glad when it was all over. Of course I had bought a quarter bottle of Whisky with me for wetting the baby's head [previously purchased] and went out to the toilet to have a good few slugs of it.

Mo stayed in Guys hospital for a few days while I went to work I went up to see her when I finished work the next day and Mother and baby were fine but she came out Saturday morning and I went to pick her and baby Susan up and got a black taxi from Guys hospital and back to our flat at Salisbury close. What I did on leaving Mo and Guys hospital on the Friday evening was I went back to the Salisbury estate and hit a few of the local pubs to celebrate Susan's birth, I visited the Duchess of York, The Gloucester, the Victory and the Globe which were all grouped together in a fairy close area although I liked the Duchess of York the best of them.

[Photo above shows Darwin st where the Globe was and Duchess of York [photo underneath] stood Darwin st/Barlow st. Mason st where the Gloucester was and at Barlow st/Catesby st stood the Victory.]

Yes I was in all those pubs that night wetting the baby's head and quite a few of my friends bought me a drink, especially in the Duchess of York which Bill and Shelia ran, my head was thumping on Saturday morning as I made my way to Guys hospital.

Anyway come the Monday morning and Johnny Donoavan, myself and our hoddie John are building 3 feet high brick boundary walls in Bagshot st when a bunch of "Little Herberts" started throwing milk bottles at us from the walkway of the Block behind us and smashed on the pavement. I ran up the stairs after them but they just ran away laughing, only kids of 14 or 15 maybe just as well I never caught them!!

So we finished the walls we were building on the Aylesbury and Ted Bell said "that's it for now lads, if we get anymore money from the council to do more work we'll contact Dave Sullivan and get you back again." We walked over to Inville rd as Dave and Linda's office was on the ground floor there to find out our new site. [this small dwelling was given to Dave by Southwark council as he was doing lots of work on the Aylesbury and I think got it for a "peppercorn rent"of £1 per week on the understanding that once Dave's work was finished it would be handed back to the council.]

Dave sent Johnny Donovan and me to a site he had down at Deptford, which would turn into a "skill centre" for the young people of the nearby area and it was a fair size site with about 12 bricklayers there and 6 hod carriers. Frank was the foreman bricklayer and he was OK but his chargehand was a waste of time but we carried on our daily work and all in all it was a happy site. We were there about four months.

Life for me at first after getting married was a complete new way of life, no pub after finishing work at night time because all my wages went indoors, I would have a drink on Saturday afternoon after finishing work till 3 o'clock closing time and after taking Tracy and Susan in a buggy down East st Sunday mornings I would get ready for the Sunday pool competition in the Tower bar on Westminster bridge rd [where I met Mo and her dad, Alfie still worked there.] There were two pool table there and about 20 people would enter, paying £1 per person and it usually ended about 2.30 in the afternoon, the two finalists would usually "split" the winning pot of money but it was great to use your pool skill to get to the final and I reached it on a few occasions so that was a few extra quid for Mo.

I have to tell you a few stories about the Tower, first of all it was run by Peter and his wife Jackie, Peter was OK but he wouldn't stop telling "porkie-pies" if you caught a 5lb trout then he caught a 7lb trout etc. He had a slight limp and I asked him how he got it, he said "I was playing amateur football and on the verge of turning professional when a bad tackle finished my playing career". "Oh that's sad" I said, then one day got talking to his wife Jackie who laughed when I said he could have been a great football player. What she said, the nearest he's been to a football pitch is watching Match of the day on Saturday night TV. She said he fell off a tree when he was a kid breaking his leg and the bones never knitted together properly.

Every day in the Tower bar about 2. 30 in the afternoon [remember it was 3 o'clock closing back then] An out of work guy called Kenny who drank in the Tower every day used to bank the days taking in the bank round the corner as Peter trusted him. Then he would come back with the receipt for Peter, well this day he never came back at all and looks like he "done a runner" with the pubs takings. About three months later Kenny walked back into the pub and went up to Peter and said "look I'm sorry I stole the money, I was out of work and all that money was too much of a temptation to me but now I'm working again I want to pay you back at £5 a week until its cleared" as he handed over £5 to Peter.

Well what could Peter say, it looked like he would get his money back, so Kenny was drinking in the Tower bar every night after work and after two weeks Peter said "I'm thinking of getting the pub painted do you know how I can get cheap paint". Kenny said let me have a word with my foreman as there is gallons of tins in our storeroom, next night Kenny said "the Foreman wants a £20 drink and he can get you five gallon tins of paint on the cheap but wants £40 up front. So Peter gave Kenny £60 there and then ,Kenny stayed drinking in the pub that night till closing time and then was never ever seen again !!!

On a Sunday night in the Tower there was a Cowboy night, where people came dressed up as cowboys and cowgirls, there was lots of "line dancing" and cowboy songs sang but the finale to the night was the "shoot out". you had a a couple of preliminary "shoot outs" then the grand final was between the two fastest shooters of the night and who do you think always took part with a six gun strapped to his leg, yes Peter the Guvnor. Two of these cowboys faced each other and when the shout went up they drew their guns and fired at each other and the winner was decided by the referee. Of course it was imitation firearms which fire blank cartridges but what a smell of cordite. The pub doors had to be open fully to rid of the cordite smell. It used to be a good night for all taking part and what ever turns you on, eh.

After the Deptford job Dave had a new housing estate at Nunhead just past Peckham and we landed on that site but it was "feel bad" job and I never got on too well with the other bricklayers there, the foreman was not a nice person and I always find its the foreman who can either make the job a good one or a bad one. Anyway we got paid early that Friday morning from Roy Motram and I went to the pub at lunch time with Johnny Donovan and we stayed till closing time of three o'clock and then headed off to Lewisham snooker hall until pub opening time of 5.30 pm and had a good drink till nine o'clock that night and went home to Mo who read the riot act to me and we had a great big row, I gave her some money but packed a bag and found myself booked back into the Whitehouse on St Georges rd again. I saw Peter Wall and one of his brothers Gerry and they said welcome back, I was put in a room for two and the other guy Keith was still there.

Back to this job at Nunhead on Monday morning and I asked Roy for a transfer to one of his other jobs and he transferred Johnny Donovan and me to a site over at Earls court and this was a terrific job ran by a great foreman bricklayer called

Hughie Baird. I went back to Mo on Friday nights to give her wages and see Tracy and Susan but after being away three weeks went back to Mo and tried to work things out. Then we got a bit of good news, the guy who lived opposite us told us his Mother lived on the Heygate estate in a three bedroom masionette, her husband had passed away and she wanted to be near her son. So Mo and me went to look at this Masionette called Cuddington and we accepted straight away we contacted the council and made a mutual swap and we loved moving onto the Heygate.

Johnny Donovan had a car by this time so I walked over to his house in Wansey st and we travelled to this Earls court job which had a "happy feeling" about it, Hughie was a great foreman and everyone worked hard every day and there was lots of laughter and singing and Hughie gave us a ten minute standing up tea break at three o'clock. See when I came to London at first back in 1968 we had a breakfast break, Lunch break and three o'clock break but over the years this afternoon tea break was corroded by lots of the "fly-boy" subbys and in fact in years to come when we had a few recessions there would only be one break per day. !! and then if you didn't like it too bad.

Working on this site a new bricklayer turned up one morning and I couldn't believe it, it was Danny McLuskey, he was one of the tradesmen I had worked with when I served my apprenticeship in Glasgow. I knew him straight away, he was about Five years older than me and we had a great chat at breakfast of how both of us had fared out since our last meeting. Danny it turned out had been in America and Saudia Arabia for a few years whereas I had been in Australia, Germany and Ireland, yes the bricklayers mantra: "Have trowel, will travel".

Life for us on the Heygate was magic and to think I had been on the building of it too !!, then Mo told me she was pregnant again which was great news, just as well we moved to Cuddington with the extra bedroom. On Sunday mornings I would take Tracy and baby Susan in her buggy down the lane to look at all the stalls. I loved the Lane and it never lost its magic for me. I loved going to Dawes st with the flea market and then all along the Lane and I would always bump into someone I knew. Then Sometimes I would take my children to the many stalls at Westmoreland rd on Sunday mornings, it was terrific looking at what was on offer, some of it was old tosh but I sometimes got tools for my work.

I remember one big tall thin man and looks like he had a couple of stalls selling everything but the kitchen sink and one day these Eastern Europeans asked him if the £10 TV set worked and his reply was "you pay your money you take your chances". so then a slow walk back down Walworth rd and when we got on the Heygate I would say "what way we will we go home?". "Will we go the quick way or the secret way" and the answer was always "the secret way" dad.

Our house door at Cuddington [1 up] was always being knocked or the letterbox rattled by my children's wee friends who wanted Tracy to come downstairs to play with them and Mo and me would leave our door opened so we could look over the balcony rail to look on the kids, although my Susan was only a baby of about a year or just over, and at the back of our flat we had a balcony and railings and Susan kept throwing her dummy tit through the railing and it would sometimes hit the head of the old Greek lady sitting in her garden down below. I ended up buying some mesh and attached it to the railings so the dummy and lightweight building blocks being chucked down below from Susan would cease.

- - - - -

Chapter 6

Marriage Break-up

Living on the Heygate was great for us and we made great friends along our block, we had Denis and Rose at the end and Jean and Peter, Maureen and Eddie in between and Jackie at the other end of our block and further along Lived [ginger] Mick and Hannah Conneely and a bit after that lived Peter Pritchard and his wife Joan. I would meet both Peter and Mick in the Kings head. Then at a later time when I used the Butts pub at the Elephant [ginger] Mick would be in there with a few of his fellow Galway mates, Colm, Coley Joyce,, etc

I mentioned Mick and Hannah Conneely as they lived just along from us and they had four children, Mark, Tracey, Elaine and Fiona. Mick and Hannah plus their three daughters went back to live in Galway while Mark still lives in London at the present moment. I was still working over at Earls court but the job was coming to an end, so Dave Sullivan transferred me and Johnny Donovan to the building of the new Surrey Quays tube station.

[Photo of the new Surrey quays that I was on the building of]

This was a great job, the foreman called Dave was a Walworth lad and lived on the Ayelsbury estate, it was nice brickwork to build the site agent called Abe was dead on, and the visiting Clerk of works was a decent guy and well pleased with the brickwork we were building. Johnny Donovan was getting some weekend building work to do and always asked me along to help him. Abe the site agent said to me with Dave the foreman's permission "do you want to do a bit of night-work Danny" "what is it I asked, he said "we need an inspection pit for the electric cables that run the tube, its about 200 bricks but can only be built between the hours of 2 am and 5 am as this is when the power is cut off. You can't do it when the power is on as there are 40.000 volts running through the cables and if you touch them you'll be killed stone dead".

So I said "yes" it would only take me about an hour and a half or two hours top whack as I would be given a labourer. Both the hoddie and me would be paid a full shift for doing this, so I was all for it. I went home and told Mo and she done her "nut" and we had another row but I said no I'm going to do it tonight [well early hours of the morning] as my Hoddie will be waiting on me. I built the inspection pit no probs in under two hours and walked all the way home from Surrey quays to the Heygate but slept on the sofa downstairs and was back up again at 6 am when Mo came downstairs and said sorry for having a row. I said "Mo this is no good us rowing all the time, especially in front of the kids" so we decided no more rows [??].

Anyway Mo and me decided to have a holiday [our one and only as it turned out] we booked up for Butlins at Bognor Regis for one week and Mo's brother young Alfie said he would drive us down there. Only snag was Johnny Donovan had a brick garage to build that weekend we had to travel down to Butlins.

What happened was I built the garage with John and got £200 for it, four crisp £50 notes. [John got a great price for building this garage] We finished the garage at three in the afternoon on Sunday, I went round to Mo's mum Eileen and gave her £150 as I had told Mo that was what I would get. Yes I know I was keeping £50 as my "bunce" ah well these things do happen in married life!!!. Mo's mum would pay our bills gas, electric, rent etc as Mo was terrible with money [I had my faults too] so that's why I gave her the £150 and I caught the train down to Butlins at Bognor Regis. I think it was about 7.30 pm when I got off the train and was at our chalet by 8 pm, it was a nice place, we said to Tracy Mum and Dad are going to get us all fish n chips so lock the door and we will be back in ten minutes, Susan was asleep. We came back ten minutes later but Tracy had fell asleep with her head on the table. I said to Mo "you stay here and I'll go to get a red-coat to get a spare key to open the door" it took me about twenty minutes to get a red coat but when we got back to our Chalet Tracy had woken up and my fish and chips were bloomin cold, so our first night wasn't too good to start with.

Worse was to follow next morning as Susan had caught measles and had red spots all over her body and face, oh I felt so sorry for her and we bought her a pair of sun glasses to stop the sun from hurting her eyes, I'm afraid this caused a row and I said to Mo "its not my fault" definitely not a good start to our holiday at all and it seems Mo moaned the whole week long, in fact I was wishing the "holiday" would end and get back to the Heygate and work.

On the Saturday morning there was an other disaster the £50 "bunce" I had was tucked inside my sock and every morning I would change socks and change the £50 note over into my fresh socks while making sure Mo never saw it. Disaster because this was the day we were going home and I took my socks off and the £50 note fell to the floor and Mo saw it !!. What's this and I said "oh its a bonus I was saving for you" well she grabbed it, I could have kicked myself. Young Alfie Mo's brother drove down and took us all back to the Heygate but there was silence in the car between Mo and me. !!!

Anyway back on the Heygate our "holiday" over and Dave Sullivan tells me that they have a load of brickwork for John and me to build on the Aylesbury, this was great news so back we went and met with Ted Bell and he said we have been given loads of money by the government to try and build garages. When the Aylesbury was originally built the architects had allowed open space underneath all the high rise blocks for people to park their cars, never realising that peoples cars would be getting broken into all the time at night time, resulting in people leaving their cars in front of the blocks or on the streets.

[Photo above of Wendover block showing all the brickwork, garages, offices that Johnny and I built at ground level, and 1st floor level oh and the Duke of Edinburgh pub just round the corner.!!!]

So we were to build loads of brick walls underneath the high rise blocks and build brick piers at the front to form garages with blockwork walls in between, so people had their own garage with an up and over door. Plus on the Wendover block we also had lots of brickwork to build forming new rent offices or admin offices on the first floor, that and other brickwork all over the estate.

This gave us two years work and six days a week and only over a ten or fifteen minute walk for me to the Heygate and the same for John back to Wansey st. Sometimes Ted Bell would get us to drive down [in John's car] to his daughter and son in laws house and build then some brickwork. We got paid for the Saturday on the Ayelsbury and by Ted's son too. Life was good.

[Photo above is of my old mate bricklayer Johnny Donovan, his wife Flo to the left and their daughter Susan to the right]

On the Ayelsbury the architect's vision was that people could walk all the way at the first floor walkways from Wendover at Albany rd [link up with the walkways on the Heygate estate] to the Elephant and Castle and never have to set foot on the pavement. It was a good idea but the Ayelsbury and Heygate never connected to each other. Of course we had shops on some walkways but not as many as the architects had hoped for. In latter years the Police would ask to get lots of the connecting walkways pulled down as this was an escape route for muggers/drug dealers.

Then my Danielle was born, Mo was sitting watching Coronation street when her water broke, I phoned the ambulance and soon we were on our way to Guys again, Danielle was born weighing exactly 6lb at 4.30 am and once again I was with Mo all the time and its such a moving experience watching your child bring born.

I went to work that day on the Ayelsbury and bought Johnny and John our hoddie a good drink in the Duke of Edinburgh pub on Albany rd just past the Wendover block that we were building the bricks on. In fact we stayed the whole afternoon in the pub as we were miles ahead with our works schedule.

Then Ted Bell said he wanted a long brick boundary wall built on Boyson rd in front of one of the Ayelsbury blocks and we had to build brick in shots here and there so trees could be planted later.

At Lunch time some days I would go into Westmoreland rd and go to the chippy beside the Red lion pub [Helen I think her name was] and get a portion of chips and a pickled onion I think her and her husband had a chippy in John Ruskin st near to the Station bar but moved over to Westmoreland rd as it was busier there.

Of course some days we went to the Fountain pub at Boyson rd and sat in the back beer garden to keep an eye on our tools and the wall as some "little Herberts" would try and kick the brickwork we had just built.

So time was flying by and I'm afraid Mo and me were still having rows, we basically were two nice people who got married looking for different things out of the marriage but they never materialized and once again I left to go back to the Whitehouse and the Wall family.

By this time Gerry and Katherine Monaghan were the Guvnors of the Albert arms and I used there most nights after my evening meal in the Whitehouse, they were very nice people and allowed me to go on the slate during the week until Friday pay day. I got on really well with all the locals and again a mixture of Cockneys, Irish and Scots. Good news was they were honest people and never added on to your slate bill.

I was sitting in the Albert arm and my pal Danny McLuskey the bricklayer I had worked with at the Earls Court site walked into the pub with another guy and I said "what brings you in here", Danny said "this is my hoddie and were doing a bit of work down Blackfriars rd and just saw this pub as we passed". Cut a long story short I got Danny to move into the Whitehouse as he was looking for digs at the time. So that was a stoke of luck and we ended up having a good drink that night and Danny moved into the Whitehouse the following Friday night.

[Photo of the Albert arms pub at Garden row/Gladstone st.]

I kept going back every Friday night to pay Mo and help her out with any bills or if my children needed shoes etc I would help her financially, even halving the phone bill !!. I'd take my children out on a Sunday or Saturday if I wasn't working and we never lost that bond between father and daughters and whether I was back with Mo or not our favourite place to go was Chessington zoo [when it had animals and only a helter-skelter or the big wheel as amusement oh and the circus which we all loved with the clowns.]

Then one Friday when I went to give Mo her money we decided to get together again for the children's sake and I said yes but Mo wanted me to have a vasectomy and I did. I went to see Dr Wetherup in his East st surgery and he said "well lad you're 35 now and have 3 children so not a bad idea and of course between you and me you can "play-away" when you have it done."!!

So a date was fixed and I went up to Kings college that night and it was all over so quickly. I was told I might be a bit sore for a few days but it would soon go, I got back to our flat at Cuddington and Mo was in tears, the neighbours from down stairs had been up complaining because this time my Danielle had found a hole in the mesh netting I had put up to stop Susan chucking things over and into the garden below. Danielle was now doing it. !!

So I walked gingerly downstairs to face the neighbours and apologize, I knocked on their door and three of the sons came out and they were all big lumps, I thought oh bloody hell if a fight starts I can maybe deck one but the other two will kill me as I could hardly walk but the lady of the house was nice, she was of Greek descent and born in Walworth so I said "I have fixed the mesh wire so no more missiles will come down" and she said that's good as we want to be good neighbours. They invited me in and made me a cup of tea which was nice and a bloomin relief, so no boxing that night thank God. I bought the lady and her grandmother a box of chocolates each to say sorry and all was accepted with a smile.

Oh and one other thing Mo asked me to get the tattoo with "Jean's" name on it removed from my arm and I said yes and I did. She had been nagging me for years to get it done. !!

Now Dave Sullivan's brickwork had dried up at this particular time and Johnny and me parted company saying good luck as I fancied to seek pastures new [I was never to work with Dave Sullivan again but didn't know it at the time.].

I went into the Kings head pub and saw a few of the other brickies there and said "any local work going around" and Joe Murphy [from Dublin] said "I'm working for the Little brothers out at Camberwell New rd/Vassal rd so I took a walk there and spoke to Fred Little one of the Little brothers and he said, "Joe said you're a good brickie you can start at £36 per shift" and I started there the next morning. It was a fair size housing estate and the main contractor was a firm called Croudace and all went well the first morning and I was put to work beside my mate Joe Murphy.

[Photo above is of Croudace's site at Langton rd Camberwell new rd/Vassal rd]

Seems I was there about two or three weeks [and remember it was a big site with about 20 bricklayers there] and I found myself setting out all the brickwork from the architects drawing/blueprints, so Fred Little was running one half of the site and I was running the other half. Lots of bricklayers will run away from drawings but I was taught how to read drawings during my apprenticeship in Glasgow.

Then Fred said to me about three months later I have a new site a housing estate starting up in Crystal Palace will you finish this job for me and I said no probs. Just before I took full command an old mate of mine Miles McGurty had started, he was a great bricklayer but oh what a moaner but I could handle him. Miles liked a drink but gambling on the horses was his downfall, when he did get a win of a thousand or two he would stay off work until he gave it all back to the bookies [I couldn't see the sense in that].

So Fred leaves and I'm in charge and have a £100 sub money float to give the lads a sub during the week and then when I phoned the men's times through to the office on a Friday morning the sub would taken from them and given back to me to make up the £100 sub float again. [remember it was all cash then] I got on well with the other bricklayers and hoddies as I treated them with respect but you always got the odd "clown", so I would say to them, "work with me or you haven't got a job here, its entirely up to you". Most complied but a few I had to sack. It was an 8 o'clock start and half four finish and only one day in hand kept and you could sub up on that day if you wanted too.

I remember the first day I tried to phone all the mens hours through to the office [remember no mobile phones back then] after breakfast in the canteen I went next door to the large site store where Arnold looked after everything and I said out of politeness can I use your landline to phone the mens times through and this Arnold made a big song and dance about it, looking up into the air and saying you'll get me shot. **What!!**

I said to him I bet Fred never had this trouble did he and as he was still making noises . I said don't worry I'll tell you what I'll do I will go next door to see Ron the site agent and tell him all the brickies and hoddies will jack up tonight because you wont let me phone the times through and they wont get paid. "Oh no wait a minute" he said and I replied too late and I went to see Ron the agent and told him the set up, he gave this Arnold a right bollocking and said "Danny uses that phone anytime he wants to phone his office he doesen't need your permission as he has mine". Jumped up idiot, so after that no probs with the phone, what's the matter with some people?

Anyway I was on that job for about 9 months and the last block of flats were built but then we had all the groundwork boundary walls to build, brick bin stores etc and lots of brick paving on the ground. This was ordinary bricks laid on their flat built with mortar, Oh Lord it was back-breaking work because you were down on your knees all the time. I was handing out sub money during the week to the brickies and hoddies but my mate Miles wanted money every day for his breakfast and to be able to put a bet on the horses at lunch time. In fact he subbed so much I had to get another £100 sub money sent down but he was an extremely fast/neat bricklayer and the main Guvnor Bill Little [the main money man] had Miles working for him over the years so he knew what he was like.

I walked to work each morning and back in the evening to the Heygate estate, I cut over Walworth rd past the Hampton court palace pub up onto Manor place at Braganza st onto the top of John Ruskin st, onto Camberwell new rd and into Vassal rd and then Langton rd, took me about 25 minutes. It was a happy job with a big site canteen and two ladies working there. Then our last bit of work was finished and Bill Little said "I have a part refurb/new work site at London bridge will you run it for me" and I said "yes no problem".

Unfortunately once again Mo and me were having difficulties and I found myself living back at the Whitehouse but still going back on Friday nights when I had been paid to give Mo her wages and if I wasn't working the weekend take my girls out either Saturday or Sunday. So I starts this site at London bridge and I had four brickies and two hoddies there under my command and we concentrated on building the new work first and left the refurb work in case it rained and then we would go inside to the old part of the building and not lose any time that way.

The site agent was a guy called Tony Nicholson and a very nice man but there was this overseeing foreman named Roger [there was quite a few sites on this big complex and my site was only one of them] and he would look over them all but what a big mouth and you could hear him roaring from one end of the site to the next.

96

He was worse in the afternoon after he had been to the pub at lunch time. He would find fault with every one of the sites in this complex although he never spoke to me directly as he walked round with a quality control foreman and shouted at him he didn't like this or he didn't like that and this guy in turn would come to me and the other foremen and pass on the dislikes, of which some were petty but others I amended.

Until one Friday just after lunch he was actually a bit slightly drunk and he was roaring like a man possessed and that's when I said to all my men "right lads everyone off the site" I went to the site Agent Tony Nicholson and told him we were going off site as I wouldn't stand for all this shouting and bullying from this Roger and I would put a claim in for the hours we were going to lose that day with my Guvnor so he could sort it out with this Rogers Guvnor. I said right lads lets go to the pub which was called the bunch of Grapes in Thomas st almost next door to where we were working.

*[Photo of the Bunch of Grapes pub next door
to our site on St Thomas street*

We had already been paid that morning and I didn't usually pay the men out until finishing time but paid all the men their wages there and then and phoned up my Guvnor Bill Little to let him know what was happening.

Well something must have happened because come Monday morning my Guvnor Bill Little was on site and said "you wont have anymore aggro with that Roger geezer" and after that Roger was as quite as a mouse and no more shouting.

I reckon his Guvnor had laid the law down to him and yes we all got paid for the rest of the day for that Friday [which made it all the sweeter].

I was back at the Whitehouse again and one Sunday night I drank a load of large Vodkas and beer in the Albert arms as Gerry and Kathy had "Charlies disco" in the public bar and I drank there till midnight. I woke up Monday morning feeling dreadful with a touch of the DT's so I thought right I'm going for an early morning drink at the Borough market where you had a couple of pubs that opened at 6.30 am to 8.30 am. I left the Whitehouse and walked along Borough high st heading for the early opener, when I got to Borough Police station a car passed me by and back-fired, well I jumped about six feet up in the air. !!

I got in the Market Porter pub about 6.45 and had a large vodka and coke straight away, after ten minutes I started to calm down a wee bit, so had another and a pint of lager and by the time 7.45 came I was feeling "normal" again and so off to our site and by breakfast time I was back to my old self again.

When I first moved into the Whitehouse it was all working men but now it seemed there was a lot of lads that the "social security" had sent to live there and I think some of them had mental health problems [God love them]. One night when I never went to the Albert arms I was sitting in the TV lounge and this lad was sitting with earplugs in and the wires connected to his shirt top pocket and with a straw in one hand was conducting the music he was listening too. Then another guy leaned over and pulled from the guys shirt pocket an empty packet of Benson and Hedges cigarettes packet, this is what his ear phones was connected to. Well he done his nut and ran out of the TV lounge.

Then Mo and me decided to give our marriage one last go, so it had to work out this time ?. I did like being back with Mo again and obviously my daughters and I would walk them down the ramp at Claydon block down onto Walworth rd and up to the Lane and it always gave me a buzz turning into the Lane and listening to all the stall owners spiel and bumping into pals.

[Photo of the ramp going down to Walworth rd, Claydon is the block on view]

And of course a glass of sarsaparilla either hot or cold depending on whether it was winter or summertime, a walk to Dawes st and the "flea market" and then a walk through the back doubles to Rodney rd and looking at the Salisbury estate where Susan was born and I worked on then passing the Rose and Crown pub where I had be known to have a pint or two. [or more] in fact many more, ha ha.

[Photo of the Rose and Crown on Rodney rd]

Of course many of the pubs in Walworth that I knew when I first came to Walworth in 1969 have disappeared, which saddens me as part of Walworth's heritage has disappeared too.

So I'm still on the site at London bridge and things are going well and we work till one o'clock on Saturdays to get the full shift and I had a drink in a few of the pubs along Borough high st as I walked my way back to the Elephant and Castle and would have the last drink before three o'clock closing time either in the Charlie Chaplin or the Hand in Hand in Meadow row and back to Cuddington and have a lay down as Mo always took the kids to see her Mum and Dad in Sharsted st at the Kennington end of Walworth.

Then the following Friday the wages are given to me by Tony the travelling foreman and I put them in my pocket, there are only seven of us working on the site so I don't check them as it looks as if seven packets are there [Usually if I had fifteen or twenty men under my command I would check to see if everyone's packet was there].

So comes finishing time I hand out the wages and would you believe it, everyone's packet is there except mine !!!.

I phone up the office and Debbie the secretary is still there and says "sorry Danny, you're wage packet is here in the office" but I'll phone Fred at the Crystal palace job [remember no mobiles those days] and Fred got his son Freddie to bring down a £100 sub for me.

I knew this would cause trouble with Mo as I would have to wait until young Freddie got the train to me at London bridge, anyway I went into the bunch of Grapes pub at 5.30 opening time and Freddie got to me about 6.15 pm and I got home to Mo about 6.45ish and because I had the smell of beer on me she did her nut. I tried to explain but no good and then when I said I only had a £100 sub she went ballistic but I kept "stum" but how I don't know.

Anyway on Monday I got my wages and opened my packet and handed the £100 sub money back. The next Friday I made sure I checked all the wages when they were handed to me. lol.

On a Friday night I always came straight home with my wages and about 7 o'clock go out and buy Mo and me an Indian take away. I left the Heygate and walked up Rodney rd cutting into Tisdall place then into Elsted st and the Huntsman and Hounds pub for a quick pint.

What a great pub this was, the last time I was in there the guvnor was a Scotsman who I believe done a bit of boxing in his time, then his wife sadly died but this was years ago so I don't know who the Guvnor is now or even if the Pub is still opened. As it seems most of the pubs I used to drink in when I lived in Walworth are now closed.

*[Photo of the Huntsman and Hounds pub
in Elsted st Walworth.]*

Then along East st to the Indian curry house [next to the chippy] I would place the order and then go round the corner to the Surrey arms pub for a pint while my order was getting done, then back, pick up my order and back down Rodney rd and have the last pint in the Rose and Crown and back to out flat to sit and watch TV.

It just happened on this particular Friday night they started showing this programme called "Aufwiedersehen Pet" about British Brickies who go over to Germany to live and work and it was more or less what I had done when I lived and worked in Germany.

While eating our curry [mine was vindaloo and pilau rice] Mo would say to me "did you do that" and I would say "yes", then she would say "did you do that" and I said "look stop asking me did I do that because I done everything that those lads done" then what happened was the brickies all got paid and where did they go to "the red light district" well Mo said to me "You dirty swine" and threw the pilau rice all over me, Oh if only I had kept my mouth closed, Ha!!

Then I'm afraid Mo and me had another big row and I packed a hold all with some clothes and stormed out the door and thought where am I going to sleep tonight, it was Thursday night, the day before pay day, so I had the keys for the site at London bridge where I was working so I went to a few pubs and had a few pints with the money I had left and then back to my site, opened up the padlocked door and went in, the only place I could sleep in was the cement shed. It was the middle of the night and I was cold so I thought I'd do a wee bit of exploring. Part of our site had been turned into offices for admin work and as I entered one door there was an electric fire on and so I sat down in a chair and warmed myself up but I knew it must have been the watchman or security guard who was using it. So after warming up for ten minutes I opened the door to go back to my cement shed when I saw the security guard coming up the stair, he took one look at me and flew off down the stair at ninety miles an hour. Next thing I heard was the police siren/klaxon and about four cops with an Alsation dog appeared and came looking for me as obviously they thought I was a burglar.

I came out of the cement shed with my hold all and the cops shouted "freeze". "Don't move and kick the bag over to us" I did this and they said "what are you doing here" I said "I'm the foreman bricklayer and had a row with my wife and decided to sleep here tonight", the cops looked in my hold all and when they saw it was T shirts and boxer shorts and socks they said "Its such a crazy story it has to be true" and when they used my key to open the door and padlock they burst out laughing and said go home and make it up with your wife. Oh how embarrassing.

I went back to the Heygate that night and Mo wouldn't let me in and so I had to sleep on the floor outside our rubbish door, I got up about six in the morning and smelling bad, so off to our site again and had a wash in the site toilets. I got hauled up to the site office and was given a dressing down from Tony the site agent who said you frightened the life out of the security guard last night and I told him I was having troubles indoors and he became sympathetic.

I went up to Mo that night with her wages and we decided to bring an end to our marriage but remain friends and I said of course. It was for the best because our marriage just wasn't working out and it must be having an effect on our children seeing Daddy coming and going all the time so after almost seven years of marriage I was on my own again. Although I still went back every Friday to give Mo her money and see my children.

We did remain friends and Mo married again and married a very nice man so I was pleased for her and I see my children all the time and all my grandchildren. I must be honest and say my drinking had a big part to play in it, see I suppose I still wanted to be free to have a drink every night after work and weekends and when you're married you should curtail it, so I take the major part 85% of the blame on our marriage break up and I apologize to Mo for this.

I now moved back into the Whitehouse on a permanent basis and would visit the Albert arms most nights after work. The job at London bridge had finished [the security guard was probably happy about this ha ha] and I was now back working with Fred Little on a housing estate for Lambeth council very close to Lambeth north tube station and was only about a five minute walk from the Whitehouse, so after my marriage break up life for me was getting back to a kind of normality. Every time in my life when things go against me for whatever reason I have always dusted myself down and said "right Danny Boy, upwards and onwards."

- - - - -

Chapter 7

The Whitehouse and Heygate

I'm still working down on the Lambeth north site With Fred Little, it's a fair size job with Fred running the job and me setting out the brickwork of a few of the blocks to the architects drawing. There was a pub called the Hercules a couple of minutes walk away and I use to pop in there on Friday lunch times with a few of the other brickies and hoddies. We still finished at 4.30, so I took a slow walk back to the Whitehouse as main evening meal started being served from 5 pm to 7 pm. I would have a wash beforehand, then eat my dinner and lay down on my bed for half an hour and be in the Albert for 6 pm.

I was drinking Tennents strong draught lager at the time and it did have a "kick", in fact one night Gerry the Guvnor said to me "do you know what Danny you are one of the few people who can handle that stuff", he said "most people have four pints and that's it they've had enough but that is the seventh pint your on now and not a bother". I said "well Gerry I can hold my drink" and then at that moment I tried to step down from my high stool chair to go to the toilet and my foot missed the bottom rung and I slipped and fell onto the carpet, Oh how embarrassing !!. another night I was in there and a skirmish broke out between two of the regular customers. I jumped in between them to stop the fight and one threw a punch at the other, missed and hit me in the eye and the other replied and threw a punch which also missed his opponent and punched me in the ribs. So that was my role of trying to be a peacekeeper over. !!!

There were two of the guys who lived in the Whitehouse who's job it was to clean peoples rooms out, Patsy McCarthy and

Peter King were their names but if you left cigarettes in your room they would vanish, this guy called Peter King was up to all the dodges going but I have to say he was a "likeable Rogue" and one winters night I saw him "smuggle" a woman into the Whitehouse, she was a small woman so he got her to wear a Duffle coat and pull the hood over her head so you couldn't make out it was a woman. I don't know what the other two guys he shared his room with thought? Or did they just turn a blind eye to it or pull the bed sheets over their heads.

The highlight of the Albert arms was once a month they had "Charlie's Disco" in the public bar and time for me to have a dance with some of the ladies in there, especially Anne the barmaid who I liked but I was ten years older, still that aside it was a good night and instead of the pub closing at 11 pm we got an extra hour [or longer]. One night these three woman came in when the disco music was in full flow, I knew one of them Phyllis and asked her for a dance, we were smooching to a slow song and I asked her out for a meal and she said OK.

Well I was all made up with myself, we had made a "meet" for inside the Albert the following Friday night and I was telling all the brickies on the site all week that I was meeting a gorgeous bird that Friday night. I finished work, went up to see Mo and my girls, gave Mo her money and got back to the Whitehouse to have a bath and shave and splash on some "Brute" after shave lotion. I dressed up in flannels, a sports jacket and tie with polished brogue shoes. I was in the bar of the Albert at 7. 30 as our "meet" was for 8 pm and Katherine the Guvnors wife said my you look smart tonight Danny. "I'm taking Phyllis" out I said.

Time came to 8.30 and no sign of my bird, then Katherine said "Danny there a woman on the phone for you" and I thought Phyllis is phoning up to say she'll be a bit late. I answered the phone and it was Mo !! she said "I meant to ask you tonight for help in paying my phone bill but felt embarrassed to ask you". **What !!.** I felt oh so deflated. I could only hope that Phyllis was running late, so I waited and waited and waited but no good she just never showed. So I went back to the Whitehouse at 11 o'clock that night in a bad mood.

I was in the Albert after work one night and my old mate Johnny Donovan came in, he said "I heard through the grapevine you were drinking in here", he said "I have a bit of private work next week can you help me out, its a parapet wall at the top of an old house, it will only be you my son Stephen and me". So I said OK John I'll help you, I told Fred I was having a weeks holiday next week and John picked me up outside the Whitehouse come Monday morning at 7.15 am, this house was over at Earls court and we got through the traffic and made it onto the job for 8am. Stephen would make a mix of mortar up and pull it up in buckets via the Jenny wheel which was attached to the tubular scaffold poles but at tea time that morning John and his son had a falling out and Stephen left. So I took over making the mortar and pulled it up on the Jenny wheel and the bricks I pulled up in a wicker basket. John took them off at the top and then I went up to the roof and helped Johnny build the parapet wall. Bloody hell I worked hard and by the time Thursday 3 o'clock came we had finished the job, John was well pleased and paid me up to the Friday night and gave me forty pounds as a "drink". So I was well pleased too and was in the Albert arms at dead on opening time in the evening, I paid off my "slate" in the pub and went to see Mo Friday morning to give her money and had a good drink that Friday from 11 am onwards.

Back to Fred's job Monday morning and all was OK, it was a nice face brick job and in my weeks absence my old mate Miles McGurty had started so we were working together, do you Know Miles was about 62 years old and I was 37 and we used to have races on the gable end walls as this was just a straight wall with no window openings in it and he beat me every time to the middle of the wall by one brick, he was a real good fast neat bricklayer and I was in my prime back then but still couldn't beat him. I took my hat off to him.

Then **disaster** in the Albert arms, it was one of the Saturday nights when Charlies Disco was playing and I had been drinking large vodkas all night long and a few pints of Tennent's extra strong lager. I left the pub at midnight and went back to the Whitehouse drunk and when I got into the place there was a steep flight of stairs leading down to the basement before I climbed up the other stairs to my room. I stumbled at the top of this steep flight of stairs and next minute was "flying through the air" and in my drunkenness said to myself "this is great I feel just like Superman" but then I smashed face first onto the basement floor and my teeth all busted. I must have made some noise because people came rushing out of their rooms to help me.

An Ambulance was called and I was taken to St Thomas's hospital at Westminster bridge where a lady nurse looked after me and I said to her [still half drunk]"do you fancy a dance" ?. She said to me "where do you come from and I said the Gorbals in Glasgow" and she shook her head and said "that explains it". So the crux was I was told all my teeth were busted but my top teeth were dentures anyway, I was told I didn't have breathing problems through my nose but my nose had been flattened to resemble a boxers nose. I then left St Thomas's and walked back to the Whitehouse, oh boy when I woke up the next morning was I sore all over and I had black eyes and a boxers nose. I couldn't go to work for a few days and when I did go in Fred and all the brickies said "is that you Danny"? they knew my accent but the changes to my face threw them.

I had an evening appointment with a surgeon who explained to me that for £2000 I could have an operation to build my nose back up again, I said no thanks, saying "I've never been a vain person so the look of my nose doesn't worry me" and I don't have breathing problems so I will leave it at that. He then said to me as I was leaving "Mr Gill do you realise that if you didn't have that amount of alcohol in your body you would have died from the shock of hitting the floor" and I answered saying "If I didn't have that amount of alcohol in my body then I wouldn't have fell down the bloody stairs in the first place". all my own fault and when Mo and my girls saw me they couldn't get over how my face had changed but that's life.

My pal Danny McLuskey who had now moved into the Whitehouse said he had a Job over at Thames television at Euston but had an offer of good price work coming up and would I be interested in going to Thames Television to take his place and I said "why not". Only thing was you only got paid once a month by cheque, so I had a word with Gerry the Guvnor of the Albert and he said don't worry I'll change it for you Danny as you are one of my best customers and I also got it OK'd with Peter Wall in the Whitehouse for my rent. So it was over to Thames television at Euston. [I will explain about Thames television in part 2 of my book.]

After finishing the Thames television job over at Euston I started working for Sean Flood, Sean had just moved into the Elephant area and had work down at Staines, Chessington and Redhill Surrey. He drove us in his large people carrier to all those sites for him from the Elephant but as its all outside of South London then they will be discussed in Part 2 of my book.

Then two things happened almost at once, first was I got a tax rebate from the inland revenue, I went to give Mo her money one Friday night and see my girls,when Mo said to me you had a letter from the tax man and I opened it [as she always did] it was my yearly self employed tax rebate and the sum was for £1.300 yes thirteen hundred pounds and Mo said I want half of it, no I said you have the lot of it because they are looking for bricklayers in Dublin and I fancy going there for a while. So I flew over to Dublin and started working for a Dublin subby called Mark Reilly who was a great lad but I will discuss that in Part 2 of my book. Look out Dublin here I come.

The years were flying by now and I was 39 years old, I had come back from Dublin after being there for seven months and moved back into the Whitehouse but the owners of the Whitehouse had been told that within six months it was to close down and turned into kind of halfway house for people with social problems, although I think Peter Wall and the rest of the Wall family were quite happy as they were going to get a big pay-out. Danny McLuskey had a cousin who was going to live in Italy for a while and she wanted her council place over in Bayswater kept on, so she asked Danny to look after it and just pay the rent each week, he asked me to go over with him to share the place and I said yes. So that was me over to West London. All in Part 2.

Mo told me she was getting married again and to a nice man who I knew, they were moving to Coopers rd and did I want to move back to the Heygate estate. ? **well you bet I did.** !!!

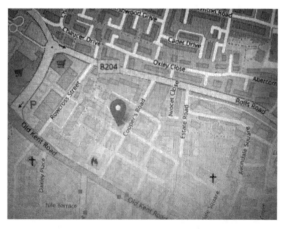

*[Street map of Coopers rd, just off
the Old Kent rd. Bermondsey.]*

So Mo with her new husband and my girls moved in to a ground floor flat in Coopers rd and I moved back onto the Heygate estate at the Elephant, oh happy days and I was over the moon. I got Danny McLuskey to move back into my 3 bedroom masionette and I kept the third bedroom free in case my girls wanted to stay the night or weekend with their old dad. It was great to speak to my old neighbours again. I worked with Sean Flood for about three more months and then Patsy Patton needed bricklayers on the Kinglake estate so I started there.

110

*[Photo of the Kinglake estate with some of the walls
we built beside the cars]*

This was the first time I had worked with Patsy Patton and we
had lots of three foot high boundary walls to build and new
brick built bin stores and lots of making the brickwork good
where the plumbers had cut holes through the walls. Lots of re-
pointing the old brickwork and it was a good wee job, our
Labourer was Paddy Dillon a smashing man. Some of the
peoples flats we had to go into to make good the holes that had
been made by the plumber and then plaster over them. Most of
the people were fine and would make you a cuppa tea and you
always treated their houses and them with respect but a few
others were awful and they smell of dogs mess was overbearing
and I refused to work in a few of these flats. Cleanliness is next
to Godliness my Ma used to always say, how these people
never caught serious diseases was puzzling to me, thank God
there were only a few of them.

On the Kinglake estate there was another builder he was called
Tom Gleeson and his men done the concrete work and I would
work for him too at a later date on various sites in South
London and further afield. He had two lads there Dave and
Mick, two good lads but Mick had a terrible stutter. Anytime he
wanted a sub during the week from Tom he would get Dave to
ask for it otherwise he would spray Tom with spittle. We had

the Duke of York pub and the Prince and Princess of Wales in Bagshot st, so usually on a Friday, Ray and I would visit one of them [or maybe the two of them]

[Photo of the old Duke of York pub in Bagshot st]

Anyway Patsy Patton would be transferring men about to different sites and he transferred Ray and gave me another of my old mates Joe Murphy to help me build the brick boundary walls. The site agent was lets call him "Billy" and every week he got Tom Gleeson to take away all the old cast iron pipes in his pick up wagon, go to the scrappy and whatever money had been paid was drank in the Prince and Princess of Wales at Lunch times. Although Tom never drank as he was driving.

There was a painting contractor on the site and he had a travelling foreman visiting different site and who do you think it was, Tony Snow the guy who had been foreman for Dave Donnaghue on his Peckham hill st job, yes the one that I told to stick his job, well he came into the Prince and Princess on the Friday where "Billy" the agent and me, Joe Murphy and Dave and Mick were. I looked at him and he looked at me and we both laughed and shook hands and had a drink, which is good as I don't like holding grudges, life's too short. Patton had a travelling foreman and his name was Patsy Russell and from the first day we just never hit it off [sadly].

112

Anyway with the great storm of 1987 there were plenty of walls blown over or had trees fall on top of them and the walls all had to be rebuilt. Patsy Patton when he had refurbished Chatham st back in 1976/7 had squatted on the spare ground in the middle of Chatam st where he used to store his bricks and timber for the refurb and he also had built a wooden cabin as his office and also built a storeroom and had gates put up to make it his place. This was the meeting point in the morning if you were been driven to one of his sites and sometimes you had about twenty men there at half seven in the morning.

Patsy said "Danny I have a great big long wall at Crystal palace to build", the old boundary wall was blown over in the great storm a few years ago so I went out there with Ray Flanagan and I set this brick boundary wall out with piers [columns] every twenty feet to match the old existing wall that hadn't been blown over. It was outside an old peoples home so they were always out having a chat [poor souls]. Anyway Ray left and I got another bricklayer to give me a hand, his name was Alan Spain, he was from Liverpool and a nice lad and good brickie. It took a month to build this wall as it was quite long and then weathered pointed it all.

We had a visiting clerk of works who wasn't a bad lad and an architect called Dennis who was a bloomin old woman but I pacified him, and when the job was being held over to the council on the last day this Patsy Russell [Pattons foreman] said to me is the architect happy with it in a sarcastic sort of way and I said the architect is over the moon and said only a f*****g idiot or a Kerry man would pass comment on it. [Patsy was from Kerry !!].

I had now been back on the Heygate for a while now and was using the pubs down Walworth rd and East st again and happened to walk into the Kings head pub and bumps into a girl who had been friends with Maggie Fitz lets call her "Cindy" and we hadn't seen each other for years, I saw Hughie the Guvnor looking over at us he didn't have to guess what was going on and my old mate Pat Carney looked at me and winked.lol. Anyway I was off work that day for some reason and after drinking a fair bit, I got a half bottle of vodka and some beer and it was back to my flat at Cuddington and an afternoon of passion with "Cindy" and then back out later that night ending up in the Beaten path pub and back to my flat at closing time with "Cindy" for more "Amore" big Danny was in the flat when we got in and he just smiled.

Next day it was back to work with Patton it was building wall that had been knocked down with a lorry, I stood at his yard in Chatham st and Patsy Russell held me a 14lb hammer and said "you'll need that to knock down the old wall" no I said "you'll need it to knock down the old wall, saying I'm a time served bricklayer and that is a general labourer's job" he started to argue and I said stick your job and stormed off. [Bricklayers are noted for being very temperamental and I was no different]

I got my money off Patton no probs, I've never known Patton to knock anyone for their money ever so fair play to him. Tom Glesson happened to pass me by in his pick up truck and said "are you working", I answered no. He said "I have a big brick wall to build outside a "naughty boys" school in Nunhead are you up for it" and I said yes. He said "I will phone you one night and tell you when its starting, probably next Monday" which meant I would have the time off drinking in the pubs up and down Walworth rd and I wasn't complaining. Like a lot of bricklayers we tend to "go on a bender" every now and then.

Mo would drive round to me on a Friday night to get her money off me and if I didn't have it because I was off work I would phone her to tell her and make it up the following week, or sometimes I would get the bus after work on a Friday night to Coopers rd and take the girls to McDonalds which was just down the Old Kent rd past the Henry Cooper pub and give them pocket money as they were now attending school and then all of a sudden Secondary school and I thought where have my babes gone. Of course Tracy was a bit older and she had started work and anytime she wanted to borrow money from me all she had to do was ask. Mo was getting on well with Martin her husband so all in all life was good for everyone.

I got the phone call from Tom Gleeson and started building his wall at Nunhead, again it was a long wall. The Headmaster of this "naughty boys" school told us not to leave any tools laying about otherwise they would go "walkies". Tom gave me a lad called Paul to assist m,e.there were only the two of us at this job, just me and Paul and it took us about three weeks to build, building up to five feet high from the pavement level and then a small scaffold to get to six feet six inches finished height, Tom laid me off then and as there wasn't too much work about I went and signed on over at Keyworth st social security at the Elephant. This was the early 90's and we had a slight recession but it didn't worry me as I knew it wouldn't last although it was changed days from when I came to London at first in 1968 and the building trade was working flat out building all these new housing estates but that was twenty five years ago.

I was now using the Butts public house st the Elephant shopping centre and it was run by Mary and big Pat, again a great pub all mixed, Cockneys, Irish and a few Scots. I met up with

[Photo of the Butts public house, downstairs entrance.]

Tommy Marks who was one of the bricklayers on the Barrier block site up at Coldharbour lane in Brixton and his brother Paddy too, we had first met on that job in 1971, Tommy was my drinking partner in there but I had lots of other mates in there too.

Ginger Mick Conneely and Coley Joyce and a few other Galway lads always met there after work and Ginger Mick's wife Hannah would at a later date work behind the bar at night time. Old Scots Charlie the cellar man from the Hampton court palace was also a regular visitor and a few Cockney mates of mine who were street cleaners would park their "mobile dustbins"outside the Butts door on their "extended lunch breaks".

When the Butts first opened it was mainly the top bar that done most business but over the years I think because the bottom bar was easier to access from the shopping centre next door, then the top bar closed and it was just the bottom bar that was open. It was a great pint of Guinness in there and there was always plenty of ham rolls/cheese rolls on sale as lots of people, especially from the building trade would have a roll as their "dinner" staying in the pub till closing time and having a kebab or fish n chips on their way home. It just the way it was and I was like that as the years went by because I found if I eat a big dinner in a cafe after work then my belly was full up and I couldn't drink. Nothing to be proud of just the way it was and the way I was.

It was a friendly pub with hardly any ever trouble at all until one night this guy came in, he had only been using the pub about two weeks, anyway he had a few drinks in him and started swearing at one of the barmaids saying she had cheated him out of his change when she hadn't. He was being a bully and thought he could get away with it, I sat there for a couple of minutes and my blood started boiling, then Maureen the barmaid started crying and that was it.

116

I was probably the smallest man in there at five feet five, he was six feet tall but I went over to him and was giving him a piece of my mind when out of the corner of my eye I saw a fist flying through the air and big Billy McLeery threw a right hander at the guy and down he went. Billy then picked him up took him down to the toilet and splashed cold water on his face. Told him he had been out of order and now the best thing to do was leave the pub otherwise he would "get killed", He got the message then just walked away and never came back to the pub again, well he wouldn't have been allowed in. I hate bully's and it makes my blood boil, I'm the quietest man going but can't stand bullying.

Of course there was another pub nearby that I drank in and that was the Charlie Chaplin up the ramp at the shopping centre beside the old ABC/Coronet Cinema this did a good trade during the lunch hour and Berna Kelly who ran the pub made food for office workers and Kathleen and Barbara were the two barmaids who worked there. Berna was married to Billy Kelly but I believe they had a volatile relationship although I have to say I really liked the both of them.

[Photo of the Charlie Chaplin pub at the Elephant next to the Coronet cinema]

I'm afraid to say that Mary in the Butts pub had parted company with her partner Pat and he went back to Ireland and I was sorry to see him go as he was good company. I always liked Mary and after a few months said I'll have to take you out for a meal one night Mary, she never said yes or no so I left it at that because sure barmaids are always getting asked out all the time. Tom Gleeson phoned me up and said "I have some work on an estate at Rotherhithe" so I went down there . This estate had been built about ninety years previously and some of the brick arches over some windows needed repairing and general making good of the brickwork. I thought well this will do for a couple of weeks. On the third week I was there, it was a Tuesday and I thought I'll buy Mary in the Butts a bunch of flowers and get them delivered "Interflora" I had only a twenty pond note left from my wages, the flowers cost me twelve pounds so I had enough money to get in the Butts that night and later on I could always ask Mary for a sub [sure she couldn't deny me as I had bought her the flowers,eh]. I get in the Butts at six o'clock and orders a pint of Guinness and as Mary gave me the pint I said "did you like the flowers I sent you". There were a couple of Danny's who drank in the pub as I had signed it from Danny.x she said oh it was you ya b******s, then she said "don't you know I'm seeing someone" and he was standing at the bar today when your flowers arrived. **Argh** !!

I said I'm sorry Mary I didn't know, drank my pint quickly and left to go to the Charlie Chaplin and after a few pints in there asked Berna for a sub, oh what am I like ha ha. Mind you later that night I had to laugh to myself but felt sorry for Mary, anyway it didn't do her any harm and she and this Steve started going out and he ended up serving behind the bar in the Butts, he was a nice guy as it happened. Worse was to follow as I went onto the Rotherhithe site the next day and Tom said to me "I'll have to finish you up tonight Danny there no more work left here", and I thought why couldn't you have told me that yesterday then I wouldn't have bought the bloody flowers, I would have been twelve pounds better off and not in Mary's "bad books". but ah sure that's the way the cookie crumbles. Eh.

Chapter 8

45 Years Old

I'm now 45 years old and the years are flying in, twenty five years since I first landed in London and twenty four since I first set foot in Walorth/Elephant, My Tracy is now working as a secretary and Susan is in her last year of secondary school with Danielle being two years underneath her.

I'm working on and off for Tom Gleeson, it seems he gets a good run of brickwork and then it dries up so I go back and forwards to Patsy Patton who usually has bits of brickwork, I much prefer the small type of works the Patsy and Tom do as opposed to slogging away from eight till five on one of the big open building sites which sometimes can feel like a "prison camp". At least when you do small building works and only one or two of you working together you feel so much "free-er".

I was working building a new lift shaft for Tom on a school at Peckham, the school must have been built 100 years ago and had no internal lift and was three stories high. So they decided to build a new lift shaft abutting to the old school, face bricks on the outside and block-work inside, I set out all the foundation brickwork and make sure it's perfectly square and drop plumb lines down as I'm building it otherwise the lift will "shudder" as it goes up and down.

Tom used a scaffolding firm lets call them "upright scaffolding" and they were based in Bermondsey, so I build the brickwork up to it's first tubular scaffold height of five feet from the ground and have also built the internal block work up to this height too. Tom phones up the scaffold firm and they arrive in the afternoon. There were three of them and the guy in charge was a proper "plonker" I had previous experience of him erecting scaffolding for me and he was just a loud mouth idiot. They erected the scaffold and went into their truck to drive away and I went over to them and said now you're taking the "p**s aren't you. They said what's the matter. I said whats the bloody matter, firstly you haven't given me or my hoddie a ladder to give us access to the scaffold and secondly you haven't given me a "Jenny wheel" where my hoddie puts the bricks in a basket and mortar in a bucket and pulls it up to me.

Oh well be back first thing in the morning with a ladder and a Jenny wheel and I said if you don't then I will phone up the health and safety and the union rep and let them sort it out. The head scaffolder said to me f**k you and they drove off. Tom had come back on the site after his travelling about and I said Tom this isn't on is it. I got a small pair of step ladders from the school and stood on the scaffold and it dropped down a bit they hadn't fully tightened all the scaffold couplings that held the scaffold tubes together. Fair play to Tom he got on the phone to the scaffold boss who came out almost straight away as he and Tom had done work together for years. He took one look and phoned up another scaffold crew and they came out and tightened all the couplings, gave us a proper ladder and a Jenny wheel, why couldn't that other lot done the same.

As this job went on it was good and my hoddie who was Paul [from the Nunhead wall job] had a good sing song every day which makes the time go in quick but the downside was that every time we needed the scaffold to be raised to the next lift the scaffold crew [no not the bad ones] would come out and be "awkward with us". So I said listen mate I don't know what you've been told [by the bad crew] but this is the story and this is what happened and once I had explained then they were OK with me. It's hard enough going to work every day without having to face "problems" that you never caused in the first place. !!!

Anyway life was great being back on the Heygate and I would get the bus back to Walwoth rd at night time from wherever I was working and have a drink usually in the Butts as it was near to my flat or sometimes I would get off the bus at Camberwell gate and have a drink in the Red Lion which was now being run by Tom Flynn and his wife Angie or over the road in Liam Og's pub which I used to use when it was the Rock bar ran by Charlie and Sylvie. It's funny how over the year hows pubs change the guvnors/managers.

Willie Cunningham was from County Donegal in Ireland and when he took the pub over he decided to change it into an Irish theme pub, with wooden shelves everywhere and books and paraffin lamps hanging from the walls and even an old bicycle hanging from the ceiling, it gave the pub an "olde worlde" feel about it.

Liam Og what does it mean, well there is no name William in the Irish language, the equivalent to that is Liam and Og in Irish means young/youthful. So Liam Og's means young Willie and Willie Cunningham did this to try and catch peoples eye as they were passing by.

[Liam Og's pub on Walworth rd, formerly the Rock bar]

Willie was a nice man and kept a great pub, Mick was his head barman and he was first class too. Willie always said when he opened a pub he would make sure it was close to a bookies shop, his thinking was a man would go into the bookies and have a good win and come back to the pub to celebrate or if he lost come back and drown his sorrows. Of course lots of people missed the live bands music/entertainment that there used to be in the Rock before it became Liam Og's.

[Photo is of Boxer Billy Knight and local lad Les Allen in the Rock music lounge, late night drinking till 1 am Friday & Saturday.]

Willie still pulled in a Fair crowd at the weekends but it wasn't the same without live music bands I have to say. Willie himself was an awful gambler on the horses and many at time I saw him empty the till of every note and rush out to the bookies nearby, some times he won big and when he did he would come back buying everybody drinks. Of course many a time he lost too. Willie did such a good trade in Liam Og's Walworth rd that he opened up another two Liam Og pubs, one at Kennington where the old Plough and Harrow pub used to be [just a few yards from the Cricketers pub] and the other one in Bermondsey which used to be called the Dockhead stores pub. I'm afraid Willie's gambling got out of control and he lost the other two pubs to cover his debts and finally lost his flagship pub in Walworth rd and the last I heard was that he had went home to Donegal in Ireland. I wish him the best of luck.

Of course sometimes I would go further afield at the weekends for a drink [just for a change of scenery] and go to Camberwell green, I remember over the years the Joiners arms almost at the junction of Coldharbour lane/ Denmark hill was a great live music pub in the back bar and it was run By Patsy Griffin and his wife and did a great trade. He had a Bentley car which he always parked up the side alleyway of the pub and on passing by the pub it always seemed to be there. He had a son who like me was a bricklayer but he was born in London as opposed to me being born in Glasgow, anyway Patsy set him up in the Rock bar down Walworth rd after Charlie and Sylvie left there but he made a mess of it [I actually worked on a couple of building sites that he was on at the same time but he was a "bit of a misery" so I never really spoke to him much.

Anyway Patsy Griffin took unwell and went to see his doctor who made an appointment at Kings college hospital on Denmark hill and he was given the terrible news that he only had two weeks left to live [How do you handle that ?]. I'm afraid Patsy never even lived two weeks, such a shock to his family, friends and customers. I went in there a couple of times after he had passed away and spoke to his wife who was a fluent Irish Gaelic speaker and myself being of Irish descent I had an understanding of Gaelic so I could hold a conversation with her. She kept the pub going for a few years but then I heard she had sold up.

Then down a bit at Camberwell green you had the Silver Buckle [previously the Tigers head] but I never liked it too much in there, it always came over to me as a "trouble waiting to happen" sort of pub. I did like the Hermits cave just along Camberwell church st, it was "feel nice" pub and I was having a pint in there one day when who walked in but "Gabby John" who remember I told you drank in the Rock bar, well his brother William was a window cleaner and he cleaned the Hermits cave pubs windows, well when the two of them got together it was non stop "yapping". I found out it was every Friday lunch time they met in there, so I avoided the Hermits on a Friday ha ha. There was no harm in them but some times you just wanted to sit down in peace and quiet and read your newspaper.

There was a pub just up from The old Tigers head which was either the "Rising sun" or "the Golden sun" which stood near to where the post office is now. That pub was a great pub years and years ago. I remember speaking to the landlady there and she told me they had great times with live music in the lounge bar but then the "good times" were over and it was demolished around 1977ish. I can remember a pub called "the Foresters" on Camberwell green but at the back of the green near to where the Salvation army place was built [?]. Of course I'm going back years now but its good to mention these pubs as I'm sure some people reading my book will remember them. I also had a drink down Camberwell rd, the Nags head, the Castle and was it the "Duke of Clarence? on the corner opposite the Castle. I never drank in the Father Red Cap.

I was working for Tom Gleeson on the Glebe estate on Camberwell Church st, he had an ongoing contract there and every couple of years Southwark council would get money to "do it up". I remember one time we had scaffolding up and repairing old brickwork and where the plumbers had put new pipes through the walls we had to make good the holes in the brickwork, it was all face bricks so we had to carefully cut out with a hammer and chisel to allow full bricks to be replaced. There were a few old ventilators with wire cages round them and looks like they hadn't been used in ages so I knocked them off with my club hammer when all of a sudden this big guy came flying out of his house and said "that's my ventilator/extractor fan you have just knocked off". Oh I said "I'm really sorry mate I thought it was defunct" just at the site agent [who was using one of the flats as his site office] and Tom Gleeson appeared the site agent "done his nut" but Tom said "no problem I'll drive down to Nationals builders suppliers on Camberwell rd and buy a new one to be refitted". So that calmed the situation down but I felt a right "wally", anyway the agent left and Tom said to me bring the ventilator cage with you and bring your hammer. There was hardly anything wrong with the ventilator cage except where I had it it with my hammer, we walked round the corner and I bashed it back to its original shape and it looked perfect. I gave it an hour and placed back this "new" ventilator wire cage. I drilled a few holes, put rawlplugs in and screwed it back to its original position and painted it silver. The guy came out and said well done mate that's so much better than it was before and gave me a cuppa tea, I felt bad about "fibbing" but it did look better and the fan inside worked perfectly so a happy ending to my "faux pas" and I made a few of them in my life time.

The boss of the plumbers was a horrible guy and I wont change his name he was called Mike Freeman, he was a Yorkshire man weighing about eight and half or nine stones but an accent that would scrape paint off a wall. He was just a horrible person and always bumming about he was a millionaire and I thought thank the Lord he's not my boss. [I would actually have a run in with him a few years down the line when I came back from working over in Ireland.]

Then Tom Gleeson had a fair bit of brickwork to build out at a children's primary school at Dulwich and I have Paul to labour to me again. There are quite a few brick planters to build and a few old walls to demolish and rebuild so that kept me going for a few months. Then as the job was nearing completion the school janitor who was a nice man said you have done a terrific job Danny [by this time Janitors were the people in charge of money matters concerning external ground-works]. he said to me "we are planning for more brickwork to be built at a later date would you like to do it direct with me and cut out Tom Gleeson", I said "thanks for the offer but I couldn't do that to Tom as he has been good to me over the years" so he said "OK I just thought I would ask".

I was drinking most nights after work in the Butts with my old mate Tommy Marks and then maybe have my last pint in the Charlie Chaplin on my way home to the Heygate. Berna still had the pub [her husband Billy Kelly had left] and I remember that some nights at one of the pedestrian tunnels/walkways underneath the Elephant roundabout this guy used to sit on the ground with his cap laying on the floor. I have to be truthful, I never gave money to these people as they always looked fit and able to me and there is the social security system in place to assist people who have fell on hard times. Anyway this particular guy must have made a deal with Berna because I was in there late one night and he came in and pulled loads of coins from his pockets, the barman totalled it up and it came to £47 **What.** If he made that every day and got his social money on top no wonder he never wanted to work!!

I was going round to Mo's at Coopers rd on Friday nights to give her money for the girls although my Susan was going to start work very soon and Mo asked me to give Susan money for her travelling expenses until she got her first wage packet and I did no prob. I was 47 years old now and how time was flying in.

I used to have a pint in the Windsor castle pub on Coopers rd opposite Mo's new flat afterwards and then have a pint in the Lord Nelson in the Old Kent rd just nearby never thinking that later on in a few years time I would live there for about 5 years.

Actually I started work with Patsy Patton further on down the Old Kent rd at this time it was just past the Rising Sun pub called the Ilderton estate just at the corner of Ilderton rd/Old Kent rd where the Canterbury arms pub stood and there was a load of brick paving to be laid and a few brick walls to get built also. His foreman Patsy Russell would pop in daily and see if my mate Raymond Flanagan and me needed anything. There were these really tall tower blocks towering over us and one day Ray shouted look out !!!. A television set came flying out a window about 18 stories up and smashed to smithereens near to where we were working, whoever threw it was either having an arguement with their other half or just couldn't be bothered taking it down to the big industrial chute, it gave us a bloomin scare and for the rest of the day we were laying the brick pavings but with one eye looking upwards. Well you can't blame us, eh. !!. we finished the job for Patton and I went back working for Tom Gleeson.

I started working at Bird and bush rd in Peckham for Tom it was a large house that was going to be made into four different dwellings, the internal works would be timber partitions which Tom's son in law Sean would do. One of my jobs at the corner of the gable wall and front wall of the house was I had to cut pockets of the old brickwork out [like an L shape] about four inches deep and nine inches high, then put steel reinforced bars bent to a ninety degree angle, then fill the void up with a strong mix of concrete which would strengthen and bind together the gable and front walls. There were three of these in each room to help strengthen the house as there was a bulge in the brickwork of the gable wall.

There were other bits of brickwork out in the back garden that I had to do and lots of re-pointing the old brickwork and Tom gave me Hughie as my labourer, he was a lovely guy about five feet tall and skinny but what a worker. Then we had a visiting site agent called Tom Scullion from Belfast and if you have ever heard the name "Tom the Liar" then he was the original, everything he said was so blatantly a lie, he must have told these lies so many times over the years that it came second nature to him, he was absolutely unbelievable. He said to me make sure those reinforcement rods/bars are the right way up ??.

He said I say that because I was on the building of a new hospital and somebody dropped a six foot long reinforcing bar [about half an inch in diameter] it fell into the new lift shaft and then bounced off the walls and embedded itself in this guy who was sweeping the floors. He said it entered the top of the guys shoulder and went through his body and exited his foot he was pinned to where he stood, still holding the sweeping brush. The ambulance came and I told them don't pull it out as you have to make sure any rough parts of the bar are facing the right way otherwise you will kill him, so I got the fire brigade out and they helped me turn this reinforcing bar the right way round and I got an award for doing this. What a load of utter rot. !!

I walked away as he was trying to tell Hughie about how he had helped kill alligators in the Amazon river bare handed, we have a word in Glasgow its "Bampot" and it means an idiot and that's what this geezer was. I just shook my head as I walked away. He only paid a visit to our job twice a week [thank God] on his second visit I was building a manhole at the front of the house and he came over to me and said are you making sure you don't drop any hardcore down there otherwise you'll block the water flow. I answered I've been building bricks since I was 15 years old and don't need an idiot like you to tell me what to do. Anyway I said I work for Tom Gleeson and not you. He then said right get a bucket of water and go to the manhole next door and flush it into the manhole as I want to see you haven't blocked up the flow of the water and I said to him go and f**k yourself.

Then I picked up my tool bag and level and walked off the job and just as I was walking down Bird and Bush rd Tom pulled up in his pick up truck and said "what's the matter Danny", I told him. Then I said "that's it Tom I'm off this job and I'm going to the Glengall tavern pub on the corner of Peckham hill st" [Yes the same pub I went to when I told Tony Snow to stick his job] as I was walking down the road I heard Tom shouting at the "Bampot" "you have nothing to do with my men, I've lost my best bricklayer down to you now".

I had a good drink in the Glengall that day and got the 63 bus back to the Heygate and went to kip. I had a phone call from Tom Gleeson that night and he said "I have a job out at Penge that has bits of brickwork need looking at, will you go there tomorrow"?. I said "of course", he said "I will pay you for today" so that was OK in my book. [see I told you us bricklayer are temperamental.Lol]

[Photo of the Glengall Tavern on Bird and Bush rd Peckham]

So I went to the Penge job next day and was there about three days when Tom said to me "will you go back to the job at Bird and Bush rd for me" and I said "yes on the condition that that idiot keeps away from me". I knew he wouldn't but I liked Tom Gleeson, so I'm re pointing some brickwork and this Tom Scullion walks over to me and said "Hello I'm Tom Scullion I'm the visiting site agent and I replied yes and I'm Danny Gill the bricklayer who told you to f**k off the other day so go away".

He tried to get a conversation going but I just ignored him. I think I was there for a couple of weeks and the job finished and Tom moved me to a housing estate just off Coldharbour lane with general bits of brickwork to do then he had no more work left so he said I have a mate called Johnny Byrne who needs some brickwork doing do you want to go to him and I said yes why not.

Johnny Byrne used to be a draughtsman drawing up blueprints for house and loft conversions but when he saw how much money could be made he turned his hand to building and this particular house extension he was building belonged to Lesley Joseph the actress from Birds of a feather TV show and she was a nice person. Johnny had Joe a carpenter working for him, in fact Joe was an all rounder and could turn his hand to Tiling, painting, Plastering, etc he was a great guy and if it wasn't for him then Johnny would have went bust because Johnny was absolutely useless but a very nice man. He would pick up a paint brush and after ten minutes put it down and then start hammering in a few nails and then get fed up and start tiling, he just didn't have it but he paid me good money and Joe. Anyway he finished Lesley Joseph's job [somehow].

I had a couple of weeks off as things were a bit tight on the building scene when Johnny Byrne phoned me up and said "I have a whole house, well the back of it to be re pointed at Stockwell" are you up for it ?, I said yes. So we got there and the back elevation of the house ground and first floor had to be raked out [the old mortar joints raked out] and weather pointed. The lady of the house who was the size of a Jumbo jet said to me "how long will you be" and I said "one week", "right this lady said I'm canceling my cleaner for a week, I'm not paying her while you're working here" and I thought you horrible person you, [no chance of a cuppa off her].

Her job was compiling crossword puzzles for the Guardian newspaper, her husband was very meek and she definitely wore the trousers in the house. I had a labourer called Tony who lived at Kennington who helped me and we both brought sandwiches and a flask of tea with us as we didn't want to ask this horrible woman to open the door so we could go to the shops. Come Friday night we had finished the job and we waited for Johnny to come and pay us, it was six o'clock and no sign of him so I said to Tony "I'm off tell Johnny to phone me up at my house". I went to the Butts pub that night and had a good drink with my drinking partner Tommy Marks and his brother Paddy joined us later that night. Paddy had given up big building site work and just solely worked on small conversions and bits and piece and sometimes I would give him a hand on one of his jobs. Sadly Paddy dropped dead on the scaffold, it was a heart attack and he was only fifty years old. Tommy was devastated and never got over it..

Anyway getting back to Johnny Byrne he phoned me up Saturday morning and said "where can I pay you, sorry I missed you last night". So I said meet me in the Charlie Chaplin pub I'll be there at lunch time, the pub happened to be pretty packed that day and I sat at the bar nearest the door entrance but somehow I missed him and out of the corner of my eye I saw him walking out of the door. I was over like a shot, Johnny held me my wages in an envelope it was all cash and all there so I thanked him and made my way down the Elephant shopping centre ramp to get the the Butts and have a good Saturday drink with my mates.

I had no work the next week so took a walk down Walworth rd and Billy McNicholas the guvnor said my brother Kevin in the Beehive want a bit of brickwork done at the pub. So I took a walk to the Beehive and Kevin and Geraldine his wife were there and he said he wanted a big brick pier built at the front of the pub and a lot of other small things done

[Photo of the Beehive bar on Penrose st which was ran by Kevin & Geraldine for years]

So I done a days work for Kevin on the pub and he paid me and bought me a pint, the following day I took a walk down East st, had a drink in the Masons but never saw Andy Storrie about so I ended up in the small Crown pub round the corner in Brandon st and Andy the butchers wife Evie was working behind the bar, what a nice surprise, I hadn't seen Evie in a good few years now and it just happened to be her birthday that day so I went out bought her a birthday card put some money inside and gave her a box of chocolates. I really had good time for Evie, a real good hard working woman all her years.

Then Tom Gleeson phones me up and says he has an old barn to refurbish but its away down in Sevenoaks Kent but his son in law Sean would pick me ou in his van at the Elephant and castle in the morning and drop me off at night time and I agree but as its outside of South London I will mention that in Part 2 of my book but as this job neared its completion I decided once more to go over to Ireland to work and bought a one way ticket to Belfast. All my life I have had the wander lust in me to travel but since I made South London my adopted home, anytime I left for other countries or other parts of London I always returned to South London and Part 2 of my book is always intertwined with South London.

- - - - -

Chapter 9

Ireland, Then Back to South London

I am now almost 49 years old and once again the "travelling bug" has bit me, I get two brothers to look after my flat on the Heygate as I don't know when I'm coming back and as it turned out I was way for a bit over two years but made a few trips back to see if everything was OK, my adventures in Ireland will be told in Part 2 of my book.

So after being away for over two years I land back once more in South London but I no longer have my flat on the Heygate, it was deemed by the council that not having lived there for a while then they would give it to someone else and no good arguing as that was it. I just hope that whoever moved in there had as happy a time as I did, part of me "died" as not only did my wife Mo and me live there with our three daughters Tracy, Susan and Danielle but I helped with the construction of the estate. Still I have the memories to look back on and that can't be taken away.

So I have no place to live, so I get speaking to an old mate of mine Owen who lives on the North Peckham estate and he puts me up in his spare room, [he was returning the favour as I had put him up in my flat at Cuddington] he lived right on the edge of St Georges way which I had passed many a time before but any time I had looked along St Georges way it had looked so desolate. I mean you had St Peters Church on the corner of Wells way and nothing else except the George pub at the other end. Then a facebook friend Peter Bonnen gave me a photo of him sitting on top of his uncles motorbike in Dragon rd [just off St Georges way] and you can see all the terraced houses that used to stand there.

*[Photo of a young Peter Bonnen on his uncle's motorbike on
Dragon rd with all the terraced houses behind him]*

Now I have to find work, so on the Monday I buy the Evening
standard and look in the construction column and there's an add
for bricklayers at Lambeth walk. I phone the subby up his name
is Sean Blackie and he says "I have already started a few
bricklayers over the phone for tomorrow but I don't know if
they'll turn up or not, he says you can take a chance in case
they don't show". I did that and I was the only bricklayer that
showed so I got the start and it was flats that were being built
with a rotunda staircase [circular brickwork] and he said can
you build radius brickwork and I said there only one way to
find out isn't there.

After half an hour he came over and said "oh I can see you're a
proper tradesman, you'll do for me". I was working alongside
Bob a good bricklayer from London's East end and we got on
well but Bob had a bottle of Scotsmac [half Whisky-half wine]
in his tool bag that he kept taking a swig from, he offered me a
drink but I declined. I was there two days and it was a good
little job but on the Wednesday night [which was St Patrick's
day] after work I got the bus to the Elephant and walked up
Walworth rd, had a drink in the Kings head then onto Liam
Og's and met up With my old mate Raymond Flanagan who

told me that Tom Gleeson had somehow found out I was back in London and said to Ray as soon as you see Danny tell him I have work for him on the Glebe estate in Camberwell. Ray was also working there so that was good news, I phoned up Tom Gleeson that night and told him I would start with him the following morning but might be a little bit late as I had to go to the site at Lambeth walk and pick my toolbag and level up and the site doesn't open till eight am. Anyway I get on the site and tell Sean that I'm leaving and he tries to get me to stay with the offer of more money but I refuse. He said come down early Friday morning and I see you in the cafe at 7.30 am and give you your two shifts of which I did.

Was good to see Tom Gleeson again there were a lot of new plumbing work being done and we cut out the holes with a Kango [electric powered hammer chisel] the plumber connected his new pipes into the houses then because of rats we had to build the holes back up immediately otherwise vermin would get through the open holes and we cut holes through the concrete landing floors with the Kango to let the upright pipework be placed in position and had to make good the top of the hole and the bottom of the hole which would be painted over.

I'm afraid the bad news was that this Mike [I'm a millionaire] was in partnership with Tom on this job, Tom paid my wages so I was working for him and things went pretty good, there were Hughie and his two sons Kevin and Sean, a guy called Dick who was a pal of Tom's and another guy called John [who I nicknamed the Fox as he was a Fox] and Peter the foreman who was dead-on, we use to all finish about 4 on a Friday and all go for a drink. I worked there for about two months and all was well until one Friday lunch time and I came back from the pub at lunch time and this Mike Freeman passed me by in his van, stopped and said stop going to the pub at lunch time and I told him to f**k off saying I don't work for you, I work for Tom, so no love between the two of us. Lol

Then Tom went on holiday to Portugal which meant this left this Freeman in charge, on the Friday morning I had to be driven to another job in Bermondsey and build 400 bricks on a wall at a primary school. Freeman who was going to be busy that day was handing out our wages [Cheque] to all the men and left paying me to the very last, handing me my cheque he said "there are you happy now" and I said pointing my finger at him "I'm never happy when I see you're misreable face" well he slapped my finger away and I slapped him on the face. A look of complete shock and horror came over his face and he ran away and locked himself in his van. I said to Paul the van driver "lets get away to this school job quick before the bloody cops come".

I finished building the school wall about lunch time and made my way to the White Bear pub on Kennington park rd to change my cheque as I didn't have a bank account at that time, got my cash from Tom Flynn [who used to run the Red Lion in Walworth rd]. I was still staying with my mate Owen on the North Peckham estate when a pal of mine Kerry Don [Yes the mad axeman from the Kings head pub] said lets call him "Jack", well he said "Jack" has a room to let out on the estate behind the Glengall tavern pub it was a council gaff he had "bought the keys off", this "Jack" had run a few pubs in Walworth and wasn't a bad guy. So I moved in there but had to share with two other guys who were a pair of "dum - dums" I was neat and tidy and they were the dead opposite. I could say a lot more but won't.

I went back down to the Lambeth walk job and started back with the subby Sean Blackie who welcomed me back with open arms. I never went back to the Glebe estate because I would have ended up hitting Millionaire Mike Freeman and the cops would have been called so I just never went back. I had a good time on the Lambeth walk job but sadly it came to an end as all sites must do. I phoned up Tom Gleeson and he said he had a bit of work down at Rotherhithe. It was a block of flats built 50 years previously and needed a bit of brickwork repairs done to it so that suited me fine. I was working on one of the corridors and as always was singing as I worked when this lady came out of her door and said you have a lovely voice and I said "you want to hear me when I've had a drink" and she replied "I have plenty of drink indoors, would you like to come in" I almost fell off the ladder I was on but said no but maybe after work and she said "just knock on the door". lets call her "Linda" Well looks like my luck had changed, eh, I did knock on "Linda's" door after work and once I had changed into my good clothes and we had a drink in her flat and cut a long story short I took her out a few times for a meal and we had a short affair but she wanted something more "permanent" and that was not for me so we parted company but on good terms. Living in the flat behind the Glengall tavern I would use the pub sometimes and the Maisemore pub just up from the Glengall and also on Bird and Bush rd. Although it was mainly the Bun house and Greyhound pubs in Peckham that I used. I liked the Bun house best it was run by Mick and his wife Rose, barman Phil and barmaid Sue, you always felt at home in there but oh dear how Rose could swear, she would make you blush but a good hearted person.

Then I got myself a bank account and because I was making good money at the time I was given a £3.000. overdraft, yes three thousand !! I was offered a ground floor part of a house in Penge with a back garden and I thought yes I'll take it. I had to pay a bankers draught of £2.000 to get the flat and that included a fair bit of rent.

I had a lot of work roundabout Peckham with Tom Glesson going at the time and the 176 bus took about twenty minutes from my flat to Peckham and for the first time in my life I employed a cleaner who would pop in twice a week for one hour to tidy the place up. It didn't really need it as I'm a tidy person but I just felt good having a cleaner.

Oh and I wondered at first when I moved into Penge would I meet up with "Betty" [Kings head Walworth rd] whom I had a one night stand with but sure that was twenty nine years ago when I was twenty four years old and now I'm fifty three and I probably wouldn't have recognized her and vice versa.

As I had moved to a new area then I had to register with a new doctor and I went to see him, he checked me out all the usual stuff, then said do you drink and I said most days after work, he asked how much I drank and when I told him he said do you know you could die anytime and I said "listen Doctor this is the way I have been all my adult life and I'm not changing now". He said "have you made your last will and testament" and I said no well I advise you to he said.

Then I came out of the doctors feeling "numb" after him telling me what he did, so I made an appointment with a solicitors in Penge and got my last will and testament drawn up so at least that me feel a bit better. [I later found out the doctor was just trying to frighten me.]

I carried on regardless still going to work and having 6 or 7 pints after finishing work I just wasn't going to stop. One thing I will say about Penge is that it had loads of pubs everywhere and I tried them all.

They had a Saturday morning car boot sale and that was interesting to go to. Of course by this time my Tracy had married in June 1998 [I had flew back from Dublin to give her away its in Part 2 of my book] Susan had a partner called Paul and they got married later in September 2004 and Danielle had a few boyfriends but nothing serious and they all had cars so used to drive round to me once in a while or we would meet up after work and have a meal in a restaurant so we could all catch up with family news.

I was working for Tom Gleeson down at Peckham one day it was on the Tuston estate that had been up for years and one of the brick built balcony walls separating two flats was in a bad state, so it was demolished and Kevin my hod carrier pulled the new bricks and mortar up to me in a Jenny wheel.

Around two in the afternoon Kevin came up to me and said "Danny an aeroplane has just flown into an American tower block" I said "Kevin according to the law of averages it had to happen one day" then about an hour later Kevin said its "happened again" and I said" Oh no this is something other than an accident".

I had finished my wall by four o'clock and went down to the Clayton arms, I walked in ordered a pint and there were these flat screen TV sets all over the walls and all showing the same thing, the planes flying into the Twin towers. It was like something from a Stephen Spielberg movie, its a memory that will last with me forever.

My favourite pub in Penge was the "Holywood East" a strange name for a pub but a great crowd of people used it and was at the bottom of my street, Mick and Di ran it and you always got a good laugh in there.

Then after being in Penge for almost a year Tom Gleesons work had dried up and my rent for this flat was £550 per month and I'm afraid I didn't have the rent money as it was winter time and not much work about, so I gave a months notice to quit the place. I had to let my cleaner go but paid her a weeks extra money to say thanks and it was goodbye to Penge.

I then moved into the Lord Nelson pub on the Old Kent rd and I have to say that Pat the landlady was a diamond, there were nine rooms so nine different people and we all got on well except for Jimmy O'Sullivan who lived next room to me who was a pain in the backside and worse when he had a drink in him.

Pat O'Rourke and me in the Lord Nelson

*[Photo of Pat the landlady of the lord Nelson after I had
finished work and the pub itself]*

My room in the Nelson was at the very top floor [once again] and a lovely clean room, bed sheets changed weekly and when I finished work at night time I could have a good drink and no taxi needed to go home. As I said Jimmy O'Sullivan was in the next room to me and he had retired about ten years previously, some nights I would come up from the bar downstairs and have a shower but as soon as I came to the top of the stairs O'Sullivan was out like a shot and speaking a load of nonsense [of course he was lonely] and after I had a shower and went into the kitchen next door to micro-wave a meal he was in the kitchen and got on my nerves so I said Jimmy I need my own space but the penny never dropped and it got to the stage I had to say Jimmy for f**k's save get out of my way.

I had suffered this for a year, although sometimes he would be in the bar downstairs when I came in from work and the meds he was taking never mixed too good with the alcohol and he became a right pain in the arse, when he got too bad Pat the landlady just looked at him and pointed upstairs, she never said anything just pointed and he got the message. I asked Pat the landlady for a transfer to one of the rooms downstairs and I was in luck, I got another nice large room with my own fridge and micro wake cooker in it, pure brilliant I tell you.

I had two pals Denis and Dougie and they lived over the other side of the old Kent rd facing the Nelson and they would come into the Nelson at night time for a drink after work and I asked where they were working and they said just over the road where the Windsor castle pub used to stand in Coopers rd, they were working for an Indian builder called "Kash" and they were building flats there. I asked any chance of the start there and they said yes start in the morning. Well I did, it was nice red face bricks but there was a language problem on the job, there were two Indian bricklayers and our Labourers were Chinese lads and none of their English was too clever [then again I can't speak Indian or Chinese !!!]. there were a lot of "hand signals" the builder Kash was OK but one of the Indian bricklayers was his foreman and a proper "sneek". Kash paid us right up on the Friday night with a cheque and I would go down to my bank at the Elephant on a Saturday morning and pay it in. I used to walk over to the lord Nelson at breakfast time and Pat the landlady would make me a cuppa and sandwich I would be singing away to make the day go in quicker when this "foreman" came over to me, picked up my level and checked the brick corner that I had just built for plumb [erect] I shouted what the f**k do you think you're doing, he might not have understood what I had said but he got the message when I kicked him up the backside. Then when Kash came on the site this "sneek" went over to him and started almost crying, Kash who could speak good English said I can't have you kicking my foreman and I said "he shouldn't have done what he did, he should have asked me to put my level up my corner not come

141

over and do it himself" anyway I said Kash stick your job and have my cheque ready on Friday of which he did. I went to the building site over the road where the subby was an outfit called "Galostar" and had about ten brickies working there.

I got the start for the following morning and when I started Denis and Dougie were waving to me from their job but not the "sneek" Lol. I gave my bank details to the young foreman and my wages would be paid direct into my bank account but I just never liked this job it had a "feel bad" thing about it. Ten o'clock tea break and I walked over to the Nelson where Pat made me a cuppa and sandwich, she said hows the new job and I said "Pat I won't be there long" and after going back on site I said to the young foreman at eleven o'clock "I'm going" he said "You're going for what" and I answered "I'm going for good, I just don't like it here" and picked up my tool bag and level and was in the Nelson bar at ten past eleven having a pint of lager and Pat the landlady said "you were right you weren't there for long" and we both laughed. Only good thing about the "Galostar job" was that instead of getting paid up to eleven in the morning when I jacked, I got paid the full day, yes a full days wages were paid into my bank account.

I'm now 55 and start work with my old mate Bud O'Donnell he's bricklaying for a guy called Tony Carr out at Shadwell in London's East end and I would work for Tony for the best part of 6 years, most of his work will be out at the Bow area of east London where I was foreman bricklayer for him on four big jobs, that will be explained in Part 2 of my book.

I get a phone call from Sean Blackie [Lambeth walk job] and he says he has a site out at Brixton and would I be foreman bricklayer for him and I said yes. It was a new job but they kept the facade of the old building and the job was already 6 weeks behind before we laid one brick, down to foundation problems that Durkan the main contractor experienced, so we were under pressure from day one. Sean and his side-kick hoddie Micky stayed with me for the first week until we got the job sorted out then he left to run another job.

I got on well with the site agent, Ebby was his name and I had six bricklayers and three hoddies under my command. We had to work flat out to get the block-work party walls up to their heights as the precast concrete floor units had been ordered to the original site schedule so no pressure for me then,eh. We just managed to get the walls ready for the precast floors but only just and me pulling a few short-cuts. It was a happy enough job and we had a fork lift to lift the bricks and mortar tubs onto the scaffold gantry's as the building went up.

Then I had a **disaster** one Monday morning going to work, I got off the bus from the Lord Nelson at Peckham and was crossing over to get my next bus to Brixton when it happened. I was at the Zebra crossing and to my right was clear and then a van on the other side slowed down to let me walk over the Zebra [or so I thought]. I continued walking the van had slowed down to about six miles an hour and hit me on my side/buttock I was spun around and thrown onto the pavement where I hit my head on a British Telecom metal box injuring my head and neck. The driver behind the van came over to me and said "do you want an ambulance" and I said "No I just want to get to work" but my neck was giving me pain and on hindsight I should have asked for an ambulance.

Then the van driver appeared and said sorry I was reaching down to pick up my mobile phone and never saw you. I said to him drive me back to the Nelson and give me your particulars which he did, he gave me his address and mobile number and I already had his licence plate number. He then drove away and I had a hot cup of tea made by Pat.

Later that morning I got a taxi to Guys hospital accident and emergency dept, got checked over and all was good except for the pain in my neck. I then got to Peckham police station and told them what had happened, they said this is very serious knocking a pedestrian down on a Zebra crossing, cut a long story short the van driver had given a "bum" name and mobile number and the cops couldn't get him. I Phoned up Sean to tell him what had happened and he said that's the best excuse I've heard for having a Monday off, he didn't believe me [at first] then when he realised I wasn't joking said oh dear, then he said go into work tomorrow and just supervise [no concern about me !!] any way I did I supervised for the rest of the week. He would drive to meet me at a cafe in Brixton Friday mornings and give me all the wages [cheques] and I would pay the lads out later that day.

The site at Brixton was at the very last floor when Ebby the agent left, he had some other firm to go to and the replacement agent called Phil was a complete "plonker" there were another group of bricklayers about four of them and they had no work on other sites so they got transferred to work there but for the Firm and not Sean and me, their foreman Ollie was dead sound. This was also my last day as I told Sean I was going to work with a pal of mine Bud O'Donnell.

Anyway Ebby the agent stayed for a week to show this Phil the run of the job, Ebby introduced me to Phil who had a handshake like a "Wet fish" and the first thing he said to me was about one of the walls being not being finished and I tried to tell him the scaffolder was coming later that day and he said to me "I don't want any of your excuses" I saw red and said listen you ya b******s don't you ever speak to me like that again and Ebby jumped in between us saying gentlemen, gentlemen.

I went in to the site office later that day to ask this Phil something and he said "when are you going to remove all the brick rubbish from the stair landing at the top", I said where about and he got very irate "at the top of the stairs" he shouted I said listen pal that's not my mens rubbish that's Durkans bricklayers rubbish and I said its a good job this is my last day on the job otherwise I'd take you outside the gate and punch you up and down the bloody street. I said you are an a******e and don't know how to talk to men decently. Anyway it was lunch time I blew all the men up gave them their wages and said you will have a new foreman on Monday[but who?] I said

I'm going to the pub anybody coming with me and they all did!!

One day when I was down the Elephant and Castle shopping centre there was this guy saying "anyone had an accident in the last three years", I went over and told him about me getting knocked down on a Zebra crossing and he said "motor insurance company's put by millions for events like this every year". I filled in the forms and it took eighteen months of solicitors sending me letters etc, cut a long story short I got just over £4.000 and out of that I received £850 as they rest went to pay the solicitors for sending their letters. Was it worth it ???

I'm 57 years old now and I was working with my pal Bud O'Donnell on a site at Kennington, which was a block of flats about four story's high and Laurence was the foreman bricklayer and not a bad guy. Bud and me were working together laying bricks and having a sing song as we built away all day long. One day it was a Saturday I left the Lord Nelson and took a walk down to East st market when I bumped into this girl lets call her "Samantha" she used to use the Lord Nelson with a boyfriend of hers but they had parted company, I took her into the Masons arms for a drink and asked her out for a meal one night and she said yes. We set a date for the following Wednesday night and she didn't live that far away from the Nelson, I was telling all the boys on the site and when it came Wednesday finishing time I was off like a rocket to the Nelson to have a shower, shave and put aftershave on and meet "Samantha".

I got to her place and she was getting ready, she said I'm nervous I haven't been out with a man for a while now. I ordered a taxi and we went over London's West end and went into the Cinema at Leicester square [£48 for the two of us] and watched the new version of "War of the worlds" then after to an Italian restaurant and a nice meal a bottle of wine but "Samantha" liked Jack Daniels Tennessee whiskey so she had a few of them. I've never been a great big eater and left about half my meal although I did enjoy it and "Samantha said why don't you finish your meal and I said I don't eat that much.

Then instead of getting a taxi home we strolled along holding hands [me holding hands at 57 years of age!!!] and caught an all night bus to the old Kent rd, "Samantha" invited me in for a coffee and she opened up a bottle of Jack Daniels and then smoked a "spliff" I had a J D with her but no wacky baccky for me thanks and then as we sat on the sofa she fell asleep and I couldn't wake her up. Oh no!!!

So I let myself out of her house went into the Nelson and went to bed, it was a good night and I had enjoyed myself all be it an abrupt end to the evening. All the boys on the site next day were asking how did it go and I said splendid. Then "Samantha" phoned me up and said she had a great time and I said I would take her out next week to an Indian restaurant up at New cross of which I did, we went into the 5 bells pub [where I would later live] and she had a couple of Jack Daniel's whiskeys and I had a pint then over to the Indian for a meal and a bottle of wine. Once again "Samantha" pulled me up for not finishing my meal and we had words, I paid the bill got the bus back down to the Nelson, walked her to her home and went back to the Nelson to have a good drink. Ha!!

Then I took "Samantha" out for the last time, it was on a Thursday evening and we went to Bermondsey to a Chinese restaurant, we had a few drinks in the pub nearby then into the Chinese where I had booked a table as it was always packed. We ordered our meals and drink and Lord she started again after having our meal, she said that's the third time you haven't finished your meal and I lost the head saying "what the f**k does it matter if I finish my meal or not, I'm the one paying for it" and the whole restaurant went completely silent, I threw down a £50 note to cover the meal and said right you out, as we were going out through the doors everyone started talking at the same time and it was us that they were talking about . Oh what a blinking disaster. I took her on a bus back to Trafalger avenue[where the Nelson is] and left her at her door storming off to the Nelson for a drink to calm me down. She phone me up the following day and apologized so we made a meet in her house for the Saturday evening and I thought come on Danny boy lets make it happen tonight, so I went to her place with a big box of chocolates and then [as I had been practising all day] kneeled down in front of her and sang "Love me Tender" Oh I made such a good job of it that even Elvis would have loved it. Lol. Then I ordered a Pizza and thought we can get in a "romantic mode" but all "Samantha " did all night long was phone her friends up on her mobile until I said right that's it I'm off to the pub and stormed out. I drank my sorrows away in the Nelson that night thinking that's it Danny the end of another romance. Then the following night on the Sunday at midnight my mobile alert goes it was a text from "Samantha" saying she wanted me to sleep with her tonight, **What!!** well I was rushing down the stairs trying to pull my trousers on and button up my shirt, as I ran along the road to her place all the drivers in their cars must have thought that man is mad.

I get to her place, she had left the front door open so I went in closing it after me, I got upstairs to her bedroom and it was a crazy set-up, her bed was six feet up from the floor and underneath was her wardrobe with skirts, blouses etc and her bed mattress was about two feet from the ceiling, and on her ceiling was painted all these physcedelic colours with yellow sunbursts and rainbows painted everywhere. She was standing in front of her bed completely naked and she had a full lovely figure, she had the stump of an old tree with a few branches sticking out and she used this as her step ladder up to her bed. She climbed up and yours truly was right behind her after taking my clothes off. She had been drinking JD all day by the smell of it but I didn't care. As "Samantha" lay there I place my arm underneath her and said oh how I've waited for this but then she fell fast asleep and started snoring Oh no!! I just couldn't wake her up and worse my arm was now getting pins and needles in it as I tried to pull it out from underneath her. So I was laying there beside "sleeping beauty" staring up at this physcedelic ceiling and thinking why does it always happen to me !!!. Then about five am her alarm went off and she jumped out of bed and said I have to go to work [she worked as a carer in an old peoples home]. I was totally fed up and never went to work for a few days just having a drink in the Nelson, when on Wednesday morning she sent me a text saying bring a bottle of JD and some cigarettes, so like a fool I went to the off licence bought the drink and fags, went round to her place expecting her to be in her nightie but she was fully dressed and took the bottle from me and started to fill up two hip flasks with the JD saying I need a drink on the bus before I start work. Well I just burst out laughing and said "Samantha" you go your way and I'll go mine and we never saw each other again. The end of another romance for Danny boy and this is the honest truth what happened folks you just couldn't make that story up.

My mate Bud O'Donnell phoned me up and said whats happening and I said I'm having woman trouble Bud, he said Laurence the foreman said come back to work next Monday or you haven't a job here, which was fair enough and I did start back at this Kennington site. Then Tony Carr had a big job starting over at Bow which he wanted me to be foreman bricklayer on and after living at the Lord Nelson for four years I left to live in digs in a Pub at Roman rd market called "The Albert" I was there about nine months when I got a phone call from Andy Storrie, he said big Davy Sherry has stabbed a guy and he's in prison he wants some one to look after his council flat while he's inside and I thought of you. I said right I'm coming over, Davy's flat was almost opposite the Masons arms in East st and it was so good going back to Walworth once again, back to my adopted home.

Tony's job at Bow was almost finished so he transferred me to Northolt where he was building houses/flats and I would get the tube from the Elephant and castle tube station in the mornings but what a pleasure being back in South London again. I will mention that in Part 2 of my book.

- - - - -

Chapter 10

Back in East Street

Back once again in East street and loving it, back to my haunts and old pals. I was drinking in the Masons with Andy Storrie and asked him how was Maggie Fitz my ex lover and he said "she's dead" Oh dear I was rally sorry to hear that. In fact I heard that Maggie had been laying on her death bed in the hospital and her son [the cardboard gangster] had been up to her asking for the money she was going to leave him. He was saying give me the money now I need it, what a terrible despicable person to plague his dying mother for money and the nurses told this to a good friend of mine who went to visit Maggie. He wanted the money so he could go into the pubs and show he "was loaded" and be a proper "Jack the lad" instead of a "cardboard gangster" !!!.

Jan and Brian ran the Masons and it was always busy with passing trade, locals and a few stall owners would always pop in for a quick drink. My old Pal Richie came in one day when I was having a drink with Andy but he stayed down at the other end of the bar as he still wasn't speaking to me [after years ago falling out with me] which saddened me. Tony Carr had transferred me to a school site of his down at Surbiton, so I got the bus from Walworth rd to Waterloo station then the overhead train to Surbiton and a ten minute walk to the school that was having a large extension to it and I was there for four months.

I was having drink in the Lord Nelson in Trafalger st [just at the back of the Lane] and it still had live music at the weekend and I thought back to years ago when Fat Lou was the MC and singer and lots of pubs in Walworth had live weekend entertainment but now live entertainment was almost a thing of the past. I would take a walk along Dawes st to the Queen Anne or just the "Annie" as we called it, this was a big pub but by this time it had seen better days but you still got a friendly welcome.

Then Tony Carr's work ran out and I was looking for the start when there was an advert in the Evening Standard for a bricklayer to carry out ongoing work on an existing estate of privately owned property's, so I phoned the number up and the guy said we are looking for a very experienced bricklayer to carry out continues chopping and changing to our houses. I was given a 12 noon appointment for the following day, the site was opposite Rye park and at the start of Dulwich which was OK as I had an appointment at 2. 30 with my bank. I went along to be interviewed and the millionaire owner and his site foreman invited me into their site office/ stores.

All the houses had been built about the 1920's and they were big probably worth a couple of million pounds each [easy] the work was to repair fallen arches and build roof extensions. Knock down internal brick walls build in steel lintels [RSJ'S] to give more space. Knock down bulging external walls while propping the brickwork above them and rebuild them and re point the brickwork [all weather pointing] and build new brick garden walls and other things. They said for the right person you would have a job for years as they had other property's needing the same work done in other areas of South London. They said they had other trades working on site too and wanted a person who could work alongside them all.

Now they said tell us about yourself. I told them I was born in the Gorbals area of Glasgow and had served my 5 year apprenticeship as a bricklayer, had worked in London for 32 years[at that time], 2 years over in Australia, 1 year in Germany and 3 years in Ireland as I was 58 years old. I said I had been foreman bricklayer on many sites had a good attitude to work and had the two best references in the world.

They said where are they and I said at the end of my wrists, yes the skill in my two hands and the knowledge in my brain, saying anyone can have written references but have they the knowledge of getting round mistakes and [no matter who makes the mistake] what is the easiest solution out of it. Also I have a good personality to work with all other trades and always give a good days work every day. I'm experienced in weather pointing, building glazed brickwork, gauged arches, Bulls-eyes etc and read blueprints. They both said thank you Mr Gill we will phone you tell you whether you have been the successful applicant for the job or not. Oh just one last thing we don't like people going to the pub or smelling of alcohol and the hours are 8 am start and 4.30 finish with only one break which is at 11 am till 11.45 am.

I went to see my bank manger for my 2.30 appointment and got a £3.000 "personal loan" which really put me in a good mood, happy days ahead. At the back of my mind I was saying if the two guys hadn't mentioned the no alcohol rule and just the one break per day then I might have took the job if they offered it to me. Anyway I'm down Walworth rd in the Red Lion pub at Wesmoreland rd and at 4. 0'clock my phone rings its the main guy who had interviewed me earlier that day. He says congratulations Mr Gill you have been awarded the job as you were by far the most experienced bricklayer of all that we interviewed and I replied that's nice but I wont be starting with you as one break a day is not on and I have always liked a drink all my life and I'm not going to stop that just to please you so thanks but no thanks and please let me get back to drinking my pint of Guinness and I ended the conversation.!!! I though that's the way to tell them Danny boy, lol.

There was an advert for bricklayers in South west London just beside the houses of Parliament, so I phoned the guy up and he said it's an eight o'clock start but you have to sit through the induction first which is quite lengthy. I got there at 7.30 next morning and had a flask of tea to have a cuppa, come 7.45 the foreman bricklayer came and said looks like you're the only brickie to have turned up mate. He said the induction includes a video and you will be there for an hour **What!!.** anyway there a few plumbers and electricians and carpenters turned up so I wasn't on my own.

The union shop steward was in charge of the induction about health and safety and oh didn't he go on, yes I'm all for health and safety but I've been in the building game all my bloomin life. It finally ended at 9.15 and then I had to go next door to the site nurse and register all my ailments [high blood pressure, arthritis, gout attacks etc] then after waiting half an hour to see him it 9.45 and the foreman bricklayer came and said to me now come with me and I have to give you my firms induction [You're joking]. he took me upstairs but was called away to sort something out and came back at 10.15.

He inducted me, gave me gloves, high viz and goggles then took me to the entrance to the site which was that big it had three turnstiles for workers to enter/exit Now he said I will get you an electronic pass to let you through the turnstile, away he went once more and came back with an electronic pass but it didn't work, by this time I'm almost climbing the walls. In my younger days on sites in London we turned up and started straight away at 8 am not wait over two or two and half hours, he came back with another electronic pass and that one didn't work either.!!! I'll be back in 5 minutes he said, it was gone 10.30 now so I took a pound coin from my pocket and tossed it saying to myself, heads I stay and tails I go, it came down heads but I thought to hell with it.

And took myself, my tool bag and level onto the tube back to the Elephant and walked into Wetherspoons pub and had a pint of Guinness to calm my nerves. Oh what a "friggin" morning but it wasn't over yet.? I get a phone call from the foreman as I had given it to him at my induction and he said where are you, are you in the cafe and I said no I'm in the bloomin pub at the Elephant and castle having a pint. I said I got to your site at 7.30 this morning and by 10.30 I still hadn't started work !!. Oh he said come back tomorrow morning as I have an electronic pass for you that works and I said OK I'll see you at 8 tomorrow morning but I never did. I hope he never held his breathe waiting for me to show up ha ha. What a disaster, eh.

I take a walk down to the Elephant at the weekend and go into the Butts pub but my drinking partner Tommy Marks is not there that Saturday and looks like there is a new guvnor called Mick a Cockney lad and a nice lad too. Then out of the blue walks in Paisley Billy [Blendon row] who I used to have a drink with in the Lord Camden and the Masons. Anyway we sit down and have a drink and talk about the old times and about characters we have known over the years and we talk about Denis Hargan who was a great craic to listen to when he was off the drink but on the drink he was terrible.

He would be borrowing money off of everyone and he owed that many people that one day he's caught walking up Walworth rd with a broadsheet newspaper held in front of his face with two eye holes cut out so people he owes money to wont see him.!! unfortunately he was murdered and the guy who killed him must have been a "nutter" because when arrested by the police for a non serious offence he said "let me off with this and I'll own up to the guy I murdered" and they done the forensics etc and it was him that killed Dennis.

Paisley Billy and me had a few pints when in through the door came, lets call him "Vic" walks in, there was bad blood over the years between Billy and "Vic". I don't know the full account of what transpired but Billy hit him over the head with a hammer or iron bar and looked like this "Vic" wouldn't live but obviously he did. Me and Billy looked at each other and I thought it could all go off in a minute but it didn't. We had a few more drinks then Billy left the Butts pub and this "Vic" came over to me and I thought "oh here we go" he said you are a nice guy Danny but that Paisley Billy and I said "hold on, Billy is a pal of mine so what ever happened between you is between both of you, and right or wrong Billy is my pal" and "if you had anything to say then you had your chance when Billy was in here". "Vic" wasn't too pleased and walked away.

153

Time passed on and I got the word that big Davy Sherry was going to be released from prison with an ankle tag attached, I asked Andy Storrie and he said he'll be home in three weeks so I said far enough . I had really enjoyed myself being back living in Walworth again and then I started working for Tony Carr out at South Croydon and got the train from New Cross gate station. As I got off the train at New Cross station at night I would have a drink in the 5 Bells pub and it was great pub and I got speaking to the landlady Claire and she said she let rooms out and so I took one and gave big Davy Sherry his flat back. Well I handed the keys back to Andy Storrie and moved into the 5 Bells pub and where do you think my room was? Yes top floor again.

This job out at South Croydon was a complicated job, it was part refurb /part new and it only justified one bricklayer and one hod carrier. So it was me and Micky Doherty [I had worked with Micky before with Tony Carr]. plenty of internal walls to be knocked down and new windows and doors built then a new workshop two story's high to be built in block-work and quite a lot of white glazed brickwork at the rear of the job. New pre-made gauged brick arches to be built at the front of the building which I built in after cutting out the old damaged ones.

In fact we were there for almost six months, and one week after my 61st birthday the job was finished. Micky, me and the site agent Del Hutchins all shook hands and I thought where will be my next job be but there was never to be a next job this was my last job. A terrible recession had kicked in but I thought it will be over soon. So I went to Tenerife for two weeks holiday and came back to South London but this recession lasted four years and by that time the arthritis in my knees was really bad.

So that was me thrown on the scrap heap at 61 years old. I kept phoning up subbys I had worked for over the years but no work at all. I went to sign on and they told me because I was over 60 I could get "pension credit" which meant almost double the job seekers allowance but I was still waiting for some subby to phone me up but they never did and that was my working days over.

Cut a long story short I lived in the 5 Bells for almost four years and enjoyed living in there, the bar had a good selection of Cockneys, Irish and one or two Scots. Sundays were a busy days as you had the football matches on the large TV screens and at the Irish end of the bar you had the Gaeilic football/hurling matches being shown and a great selection of bar food for all the customers given out free. On Saturdays when Millwall were playing at home the pub was packed with Millwall fans and I got to know a few of them and looked forward to our chats. Seamus and Bridget were the owners but really it was their eldest daughter Claire who ran the pub with her sisters Bernadette and Louise.

[Photo of the 5 Bells pub at New Cross]

They had a terrific barman called Bill Long, he could serve everyone even when the pub was packed, he always remembered what you drank and would sing funny songs while working behind the bar and regale us all with jokes. In fact I said to him one day "Bill, you are the second best barman in the world" he said alright who is the best one Danny and I replied "I haven't met him yet"Lol. One thing I have noticed in my lifetime is that if went into into a bar and the barman/maid was miserable then I'd only have the one drink and leave but if the barman/maid was nice and cheery then I would stay and have another drink its human nature.

As I say Bill was a great barman and one evening these two "toe-rags" came in ordered a drink and then went to the toilet came back to the bar picked up their pints and tried to sit down without paying for their drinks when Bill said now come on lads its a nice sunny evening outside, everyone is in a good mood so don't upset the apple-cart, the two toe-rags tried to blame each other for not paying and Just at that moment one of the locals left to go to the bookies and as the door was closing behind him Bill quick as a flash shouted get out of here you tried to get off without paying for a drink before, you're barred get out before I set the Alsation dog on you. These two toe-rags turned round and saw the closing door and though Bill had scared him off with the threat of the dog, these two "Herberts" promptly paid for their drinks and left, wasn't that brilliant, Bill had got rid of two undesirables without breaking sweat, that's what made him the second best barman in the world.

Anyway getting back to my knees, the climbing of the stairs up to my room on the top floor was killing my knees and by this time I was using a walking stick as some days when out and about my knees could just"go" on me. I always thought that I would be building bricks up to and into my seventies but this wasn't to be. I honestly think that if it wasn't for that terrible recession I could have worked through the pain of the arthritis in my knees but after being out of work for so long my knees had "seized" up, although I was philosophic about it and thought ah well if I'm retired then I will make the best of it.

The pub cleaner was called Maggie and she kept saying to me "Danny you're over 60 now you can get sheltered housing but I wasn't too sure of how you went about that. Then I saw there was this kind of citizen's advice place opposite the 5 Bells pub so I went over there to enquire and the person I saw said no chance but you can get "disability allowance" so I made an appointment and was told it was an "open office" and first come first served. The office opened at 9 am but if you were first in the line outside the office you would be seen first, so come the Friday morning I started queuing up outside the office at 7 am to be first. I got in and sat down and this guy made an appearance and said can I help anyone with a housing request and I though why not and said yes please.

He sat me down and I told him I had been a bricklayer all my life, I now suffer from arthritis in my knees and live four floors up which kills me. I also said I was on heart meds for high blood pressure and do you know what within seven weeks of seeing this guy I had moved into Sheltered housing out at Lee green [Lewisham].

I was invited by Lewisham council [or Lewisham homes as they re now called] to meet one of their officer and she would show me over the flat. It was December 2010 and so bitterly cold, I was waiting outside this sheltered housing block of flats when somebody went out and I went in and stayed in the warm and the heat hit me straight away [luvly jubbly]. The Lady officer from Lewisham homes came about half an hour later and took me to my door and opened it, it was a terrific little self contained flat, a fair sized front room, small kitchen, a box room which I could use as my bedroom and a bathroom with a walk in shower and it faced the main street with plenty of light coming in through the window.

She said I'll let you think about it for five minutes before you decide and I said No!!!, I'll take it and I did. I went back to Lewisham homes office, signed all the paperwork and was now a tenant of my own "Palace". of course I stayed in the 5 Bells pub for the last week while getting a fitted carpet laid in my new home, then got the necessary's like a fridge, cooker bed/mattress, wardrobe, curtains etc. Then on the Saturday morning I left the 5 Bells and moved into my "Palace" Claire and her family bought me a micro wave oven as a going away present. wasn't that nice of them.

[Photo of me standing outside my sheltered housing "palace" taken in 2020]

It was a bad winter that year with plenty of snow blizzards and sub zero temperatures but my flat had central heating and I was so warm. My first day there and the lady next door from me met me in the hallway and lets call her "Mary" and she said welcome which was nice and she gave me the "run down" on the block of flats where I now live which again I though was nice, then she said do you like a drink and I said oh yes I do, I said I drink either Guinness or Fosters lager.

Next day she knocked on my door and said I'm having a drink indoors, care to join me and to be sociable I sad yes. She had bought a carton of Fosters and put it in her fridge so we sat down and had a drink and she told me she had come from Gaywood st on St Georges rd at the Elephant and I told her I had lived and worked at the Elephant and Walworth for many many years, so we had something in common to discuss and I thought this was nice but I later regretted it immensely because it seemed she was knocking on my door all the time. I would go out in the morning to have a walk and down to Sainsbury's supermarket only a twenty minute walk away, well I would walk there but get the bus back, before I left I would go to her door [which was always left wide open] I always asked her did she need anything and away I went I would come back and read the newspaper I had bought in my flat then take it into her in the afternoon but when I gave her the paper "Mary" was very merry after drinking and would invite me to have a drink. I did the first couple of days but then it was getting too much. I said I do like a drink but like to leave it till the evening time now. I had made the mistake of giving her my mobile number and she then started sending me texts, saying I haven't saw you all day are you alright and come into my flat for a drink.!!

I said no I'm reading a book or listening to the music on the radio but she wouldn't have it and then came knocking on my door and when I didn't answer she would be pushing little notes through my letterbox and I thought to myself this is like that film "Fatal attraction" but without the sex ha ha.

This went on for the best part of five months and I thought how do I get out of this, basically she was a nice lady who wanted company but I wanted to be on my own and enjoy my retirement at my own leisure and not be having to keep opening the door to her all hours of the day so at the end up I said "Mary" this has to stop as I need my own space and she said sorry. Anyway I made a"deal" with her saying come into my flat the last Sunday of the month and I'll have a bottle of Vodka and we can sit and have a talk for a couple of hours. That was fine for the next couple of months until the "little notes" started coming through my letterbox again and I said that's it no more.

Now I hardly ever see her, only in the passing of each other in the hallway when I always say hello bu that's it and as for the other neighbours well some of the poor souls need carers to look after them daily and with others its a "one way conversation" so I just keep to myself and I have lots to do with writing my books [mainly about the Gorbals area of Glasgow where I come from] or listening to music on my CD's or radio then switching on my TV at 6 pm and watching the news then the following programme's and at 7.30 have my first beer of the day from the fridge and life couldn't be better for me. I worked really hard all my life so now I want to live it at a leisurely pace.

I used to go out to Wetherspoons pub twice a week, Tuesdays and Fridays but since this covid-19 virus [as I write] I don't go out to pubs at all, just take a slow walk round the block for a bit of exercise. Although my daughters will pick me up in their cars and we have a family gathering with all my grandchildren in one of mt daughters gardens while observing social distancing.

My life nowadays is not as exciting as it was when I was building bricks and travelling from site to site and even other countries and my love life is now left to my memory but some terrific memories ha ha. Life has been extremely good to me and I have so much to be thankful for and also I'm glad that I made Walworth my adopted home but when I die my daughters will take my ashes back to the Gorbals to be scattered outside of St Francis's Church where my Ma and Da were married and I was baptized.

But for you the reader my story doesn't end here,

Far from it because in Part 2 of my book I tell you about all the other events in my life while I was working, overseas and other parts of London outside of South London and all the many happy/sad and tragic events that happened to me. So hold on my roller coaster life continues.

- - - - -

Part 2

Lifetime and adventures of a Gorbals Bricklayer overseas and outside of South London.

Chapter 11

King's Cross London/King's Cross Sydney

I landed at Euston railway station in September 1968 from Glasgow without knowing a soul in the world and this was to be the start of my lifetime and adventures, it was a Sunday morning and first thing I done was put my suitcase/tool bag and spirit level into the left luggage place and then had a cuppa tea in the railway station. After that I took a walk down to Kings cross railway station as there seemed to be lots more "life" there. I looked in shop windows which advertised rooms to let, it gave the address and price of the room but I just didn't know any of the streets at all as I was a complete stranger. So I walked and walked and found myself in Argyle square just at the back of Kings cross and there was this "hostel" that had a notice in the window advertising a place to stay for £5-15/- per week, I went in and saw the guy in charge and he showed me the room, it was 6 single beds, no wardrobe or chest of drawers but I was desperate for a place to stay so I took it.

He told me there was a Sunday lunch served but that was the only food of the week, there was always a giant pot of tea on the go so you could drink as much tea as you wanted and if you wanted a call in the morning for work then you marked your bed number and what room you were in on a blackboard with a piece of chalk a and a guy would give you a call in the morning. [Is this really the swinging 60's I thought to myself ?] Anyway I took it and paid the guy, then took a walk back to Euston railway station and retrieved my suitcase and tools and went back to my "digs" and put them under my bed, the guy running the "hostel" told me they would be safe there as he kept his eye on everyone entering and leaving. Comes two o'clock that day and lunch was served in the lounge and the food was OK, there was about 30 of us all sitting there and after lunch the TV set was turned on for "match of the day" which showed a couple of yesterdays football matches. Then I went and laid on top of my bed for an hours kip and up that night for my first pint in a London pub, it was the Duke of York on Caledonia rd and I had a pint of Guinness, then walked back to my digs and there was a pub just on the corner which was called the Prince of Wales and this would become my local pub.

Next day Monday morning I bought the Evening news newspaper as they had adds in it for the building trade jobs [I had asked the barman in the Prince of Wales about adds for the building trade]. I was gobsmacked as the building trade section had hundreds of jobs advertised for Brickies, Chippy's, Plasterers, Electricians, Painters etc. In fact there were 89 jobs advertised for bricklayers alone because at that time London was going through a massive redevelopment for houses, office blocks, etc. I phoned the first advert and it was for Brickies out at a place at Hatch end and was told it took 25 minutes on the train from Euston and a five minute walk to the site, so I said "yes I'll be there in the morning". I was so excited this was to be my first job in London and I landed on the site the next morning at eight o'clock.

I saw the foreman bricklayer called Clive and he was OK, there were four bricklayers and two hoddies and it was three story high flats we were building, face bricks outside and block work inside. Everything went smooth and on the Friday came pay day, they held one day in hand so because I had started Tuesday morning I got paid Tuesday, Wednesday and Thursday but Clive told me I could have a "rhubarb" and I said "whats a "rhubarb" as I wasn't hungry and he laughed and said its Cockney rhyming slang for =rhubarb tub = sub". So I could sub part of Fridays money and I said "yes I'll have a "rhubarb". My wages were £4.10/- per shift which meant I got paid £22. 10/- for the full five days which was OK as my money in Glasgow had been roughly £20 per week.

We had three tea breaks per day on site, tea break at 9.30 am and lunch at 12,30 and afternoon tea at 3 in the afternoon, which I thought was terrific. Anyway this Clive asked me where I was from and I replied "Glasgow and again he laughed and said no where about in London" ? "Oh I said Kings cross and he said you're travelling too far, there's plenty of work all over London no matter what area you came from and he said to me get yourself a site near to Kings cross although I'll be sorry to see you go". I thought about this but decided to stay put for the time being as I was just getting on my feet, so I stayed there for a month then got work a bit nearer to Kings cross and left.

I started on a new site not far from Kings cross and again it was with a nice bunch of lads and by this time on the weekends I was gradually finding what buses to get and going on the tube and after making many mistakes was slowly getting the hang of getting about but when you're a complete stranger to a new city it all takes time. I was in this "hostel" and I didn't like this 6 in a room with guys snoring and breaking wind all night long. While having a few pints in the Prince of Wales pub [pub beside me] I got speaking to this guy called Bob who was a Chef and came from Manchester and he seemed OK [Turned out to be scum bag] and he also lived in my "hostel" but in a different room and we got to become friendly.

By this time I had started work on Perronet house at the Elephant &Castle which was only about fifteen minutes away on the bus and was enjoying working there. All of a sudden it's Christmas time and I went back to Glasgow for the New Year and was great being back in my home city again but as soon as the New year celebrations were over it was back to London and back into this "hostel" I booked back in for a week but then this Bob the Chef and me decided to leave and move across the street to the "sixty hotel" which was a bed and breakfast place, we shared a room, just a single bed each and wardrobe and chest of drawers for our clothes and a wash hand basin in the room and a bathroom/shower next door, we both paid £5 per week. I was well pleased and I would have my evening meal in a local cafe after work then go home to read a book at night time in my room while Bob preferred going to the pub every night.

All of a sudden it's nearing the 11th of January which will be my 21st birthday and I have just become an uncle as My sister Jeanette gave birth to my nephew David. I go to work at Perronet house and Friday I get paid and have a real good drink that night as I'm preparing myself for my 21st birthday tomorrow on Saturday. I go to work on the Saturday morning [my 21st] and we only work till one o'clock and get paid the full shift, only thing was because my head was a bit fuzzy with the previous nights drink I had left my wallet with my wages in it, in the drawer beside my bed but sure I'll get that when I get back to my digs. I had about £1 loose change on me to pay for my bus fare to work and buy breakfast, so I get back to my hotel room all excited, I'm going to have a bath and have a few beers then have a kip and go out in the evening to celebrate my 21st birthday properly.

I get back to my room and **Disaster** I go to my bedside drawer and my wallet with all my money in it had gone, I was completely devastated this Bob had stolen my money, he was gone and his suitcase had gone, what a terrible awful thing to do to your roommate. I felt like crying I just lay on top of my bed and cursed him, everyone should have special memories of their 21st birthday but unfortunately not me. I had a bath later and did go out to celebrate, out of the £1 loose change I had about 11 shillings left so I went to the Pinder of Wakefield pub on Grays Inn rd about a five minute walk from my hotel/digs and had three pints of Guinness and a packet of cheese and onion crisps while watching Raymond Burr as Ironside on the TV in the pub, I didn't want to go into my local pub the Prince of Wales as I didn't want to face the people I knew in there as I would be so embarrassed to tell them what happened. Yes I will never ever forget my 21st birthday that's for sure and as for that guy Bob well I have always been a great believer in Karma and somewhere along the line in his lifetime he would come unstuck.

I stayed in my room on Sunday the following day and read a book, then on Monday went to work at Perronet house and got a sub off Pat the foreman bricklayer and the following Friday I went in to the Prince of Wales pub to tell the people I had become friendly with what had happened and all my Cockney pals were disgusted on hearing what had happened to me. Worse thing was that Friday night when I went to pay my £5 rent money to Frank the manager of the 60 hotel, he said Danny "it has to be £10 you pay me as its a for two people" and even although Bob has gone I must have £10 for the room. Which made me see red again as this Bob has cost me more money. I told this to Nell and Bob who lived in a council block of flats next door and were people I had a drink with in the Prince of Wales and Nell said "no come live with us we have a spare bedroom and we can put you up". That was brilliant and I paid Nell and Bob £10 per week but with that got an evening meal every night and all my washing done and sat in every night watching Tv and cups of tea and biscuits. I had now been in London for eight months and got a wee bit homesick so decided to leave Nell and Bobs and also left Perronet house that I was working on and went back to Glasgow to see my Ma and Da, sister and baby nephew and my old mates. Although I returned to London a few months later with another bricklayer called Bobby Morrison and would finally set foot in Walworth and South London.

Manchester

After staying at our digs at Grays Inn rd and working with George Batt at Holborn, Bobby Morrison and I saw an advert for bricklayers up in Manchester and decided to travel there. It was a large extension to an engineering factory and the guy who owned the factory picked us up in his pick up truck and dropped us off at a pub which was to be our digs. It was at a place called Bollington near to Macclesfield, the pub we stayed at was a nice place and we got breakfast and evening meal and had the use of the shower/bathroom and had a drink there every night and no need for a taxi home.

Only thing was Bobby and me were living in each others shoes, we were working together, drinking together and sharing the same bedroom although we had single beds and it all got on top. We finished the job for the guy, then Bobby and me decided to part company I think Bobby went back to Glasgow while I headed back down to South London.

King's Cross Sydney

I had left Maggie Fitz behind in South London and got a flight to Sydney Australia, I landed at Sydney airport once again without knowing a soul in the world but this was all part of my adventures to me. I landed with £200 sterling and at the airport I went to the hotels desk and was booked into the Chevron hotel at $16 dollars per night and I actually shared a taxi from the airport with Liverpool comedian/singer Johnny Hackett as he also had booked into the Chevron hotel. We were staying in next door rooms, so after me hanging my clothes up this lad Johnny Hackett knocked on my door and said fancy a drink lad and I said yes and so off we went for a few hours to breathe in the air and have a few beers. At first I never knew that Kings cross here in Sydney was the red light district but looking around I could easily spot all the hookers standing about and there were so many night clubs, strip joints etc there and the place was packed with people as this is the place where it all "happened" there was such a buzz about the place. After a few beers we returned to the hotel and I said goodnight to Johnny and never saw him again.

So in the morning I woke up and pulled back the window curtains and in front of me about a mile away was the Iconic Sydney harbour bridge and such a sight in the morning sunlight. Right what do I do, well first of all find out the lay-out of the land and so I found out what buses to get into Sydney city and trying to get my head round the Australian accent. I have a couple of beers in the bars in the city and they have a counter lunch service in the city bars, it was great value and for $1. 50cents you had a lovely lunch just sitting at the bar or sitting at one of the tables and in the evening it was the same for a counter tea, again another good meal and so cheap. I took a trip down to the Sydney harbour bridge and then not far away took a walk around the Sydney Opera house and then that was me I had seen them so they were no more a novelty to me. I suppose its like when Americans and other tourists come to London they flock to Big Ben and Buckingham palace, etc.

So I've been in Sydney for about a week now and have a rough idea of the lay out, that's when I started using the Kings cross hotel pub and Kelly the barman [Australian born n bred] and me got talking and he said what brings you here and I said well I always fancied coming to Oz as its the land of sunshine and opportunity. Kelly says oh yes well we do get the sunshine alright but at the moment the state of New South Wales is going through a bad recession and there's hardly any work about. **What** I said !!! oh yes Kelly said no work mate, oh bloody hell what have I done., I told him I was a bricklayer looking for work and he said you'll be lucky as the good days have gone [for now anyway]. He asked me where I ws staying and I said the Chevron hotel at $16 per night and he said why don't you stay here its $16 per week and "mother" who runs it has spare rooms upstairs so I went upstairs to see "mother" and she said yes move in and I was round like a shot to the Chevron to settle up my bill and moved into the Kings cross hotel or the KC as it was sometimes nicknamed.

When I had landed in Sydney I had £200 but that was now down to £90 after paying my hotel bill and having a drink every day in the bars, the newspaper for building jobs was the Sydney morning Herald and it came out at three am. So every morning at three I went out and got the newspaper to see if they were looking for any bricklayers but no and it was like that for the next three weeks and my money was fast dwindling, I paid "mother" two weeks in advance and again my money is fast disappearing. I think to myself I should have checked up before I left London that there was work for bricklayers in Sydney but I always thought Australia was the land of opportunity. Then I had a break there was an advert for a bricklayer in Monday mornings edition of the Sydney Morning herald and so I got my tool bag and level and got a taxi to the address. It was a school they were building and the taxi ride cost me $13 dollars, so I gave the driver a $1 dollar tip and that was me left with $6 dollars from my last $20 dollar bill and this $6 was all the money I had left in the world. I was sitting there under the moon as I had got to the job at four am and by the time it was seven am there was a queue of eight bricklayers behind me, yes it sure looked like a recession was on. It was an Italian subby and he said first one please, as I walked with him I looked back and the other brickies were still sitting there and obviously if I was no good then it would be "2nd in line please".

This Italian subby looked at me as I was wearing long trousers and everyone else was wearing shorts and my face wasn't very suntanned and he pointed to the face bricks already built and said can you build bricks as good as that and before I could answer he said I will give you an hours trial in his broken English. I thought right ya swine I'll show you how to build bricks, he said I will build this corner and you build the other corner and I started working quickly and I had my corner built and finished as he only had his half built. He came over to me and said Slowa downa, slowa downa you've passada the test. There were four Italian bricklayers and one Italian labourer and we all got on well, their English wasn't too good and neither was my Italian but we got through with hand signals and they couldn't figure out how I could sing away and build bricks at the speed I did.

I got paid that Friday and was paid up to the Friday night at $50 per shift all cash, oh happy days. First thing I did with my wages was buy a pair of shorts as it was murder working in long trousers in this heat, it was a 7.30 am start and 3.30 finish and I opened up a bank account and I thought this is more like it Danny boy. I was at that site for four weeks when we caught up with the concreters concreting the floors. My boss Luigi said I have to lay you off and was almost crying and said will you please come back when the concreting is all finished and I sad yes but never did [which I'm sorry for as I liked all those lads] I happened to get a start on a job in Sydney city centre and by this time my legs were all bronzed as were my arms so no laughing at my milk bottle legs which happened when I first wore my shorts.

There was this guy called Jimmy Thomson who also lived in the Kings cross hotel he was from Manchester aged 49 but had been in Oz since he was 19. He said to me where are you working and when I told him he said I work in a Bistro bar opposite as a kitchen porter and he said that he and Trudy the New Zealand barmaid in the Bistro bar took their break from 3.30 till 5 in the pub along a bit did I fancy joining then when I finished work of which I did. I finished at 3.30 and went upstairs to the lounge bar as women weren't allowed to use the public bars at that time [but could work as barmaids in them ?]. Anyway this Trudy was a part Maori with a lovely chocolate brown colour, more like a Polynesian I thought and she was drop dead gorgeous, seems we met every day and Jimmy said why don't we all go out for a drink on Sunday.

At that time in Sydney pubs didn't open on a Sunday but clubs did and Jimmy was a member of one of these clubs so we all went along, we had a great day in there listening to the live band music and after about 6 hours of drinking in there Trudy said will you take me home and I surely did. She was sharing a flat with another New Zealand girl called Carol but I don't think they were getting on too good. Cut a long story short Trudy and me slept together that night and what a night of passion [oh la la]. In the morning we continued our love making then I had a shower and went to work smiling, Trudy and me were the same age 26. Jimmy said why don't we all share a flat together as Trudy wasn't getting on with her flat mate Carol and so we moved into a ground floor flat a five minute walk from the Kings cross hotel. At first things were OK but then I found out that when Trudy drank she became a "nutter".

I was working on a new site which was out in the sticks so we started at 6.30 am and finished at 2. 30 because to be truthful the sun was so hot then that I was glad of the early finish and there was this Australian hoddie on the job who lived near me

170

so he picked me up in his car in the morning and dropped me off at Kings cross after we had finished. I would go straight into the Kings cross hotel pub or KC as we called it and it was nicely air conditioned and slake my thirst. I was in there one day after work and this guy came walking over to me and said it's Danny Gill isn't it and I said good God its Jimmy O'Neill, Jimmy and me had been working together in Glasgow as bricklayers in 1968 after I had finished my apprenticeship but I hadn't been down to London yet. Well Jimmy and me had a good old drink that day and he told me that when he had come to Australia at first there was so much building work going it that it was great but said now we have a recession but seem to coming out of it. I never laid bricks with Jimmy in Sydney but we did meet up in the KC and have a good drink many a time.

After I left the KC after work I would go home have a shower and have something to eat watch a bit of TV and would get to bed by 10 am but this was the time that Trudy and Jimmy finished work so they would come in about half ten or eleven and want to start drinking beer from the fridge or vodka as that's what Trudy drank and they would waken me up, so sometimes I would get up and join them but then Trudy started arguing for no reason at all, she just went nuts. Then she would calm down and I would go into her bedroom and we made love and then all of a sudden it was 5 o'clock and time for me to get up for work although my car ride to the site wasn't till 6 am but I liked to have a shower and cup of tea.

Then Trudy told me that Jimmy was running me down behind my back, truth be told he was jealous of me and Trudy making love, well he was almost double our age. It came to a head one might after they had come in at eleven o'clock and jimmy kept drinking beer after beer from the fridge and then he went into the kitchen and I herd this clunk, clunk, clunk it was Jimmy dropping ten cent coins into the gas meter and then he stuck his head in the gas oven to try and gas himself but it was all pretend. Trudy said what's that noise as Jimmy had dropped the coins into the gas meter and I had said Jimmy's trying to gas himself and she ran into the kitchen and let out a scream.

171

So we pulled him bodily away from the gas oven and he was all groggy saying I'm sorry, I'm sorry then I threw a bucket of water over him and me made a "miraculous recovery" but he left the flat the next week and moved back into the KC. A week later Trudy got a telegram saying her Dad wasn't well and she flew back to New Zealand, but he made a recovery but one night Trudy got drunk and tried to "slit her wrists" but only a half-hearted attempt and I thought bloody hell he's tried to gas himself and now she's tried to cur her wrists. Anyway I had been in Sydney for a year and Trudy and me decided to go down to Melbourne to live, so we got the overnight sleeper train from Sydney central railway station to Spencer st railway station in Melbourne. We got a ground floor flat at a place near to an area called St Kilda and it was bloomin cold, everyone thinks Oz is always hot but in Melbourne in their winter time its really cold and wet.

So I started work with a German subby called Joe Schmitt about three miles away and meet up with another Glasgow brickie called Charlie O'Donnaghue and there was an Italian brickie, a Yorkshire brickie and old Scottish brickie from the Highlands, a German labourer and a Greek labourer, talk about the league of nations but we all got on well together. We had been there about two weeks in Melbourne and Trudy and I were getting very close and making love every night, she hadn't got a job yet but sure I was getting a wage every week. Then another **Disaster.** I came home on the Friday night with my wages walks into our flat and Trudy is sitting there drunk with another guy and I said who's this and she said this is Johnny [who was also drunk] and he lives next door and just at that second the TV that was switched on started showing "Flipper" the song started "Everyone loves the king of the sea" I looked at the two of them and said to Trudy well f**k you, f**k Johnny and f**k Flipper and stormed off out and went to a pub. I came back that night but no sign of Trudy, she must have been with Johnny. I went to bed but took my wages and put them inside my boxer shorts and fell asleep, then about two in the morning I woke up and Trudy had been in the flat as my wallet was laying opened on the floor, she had been looking for my wages, then there was a movement outside of my window it was Trudy in her pink nightie kneeling on the road outside our flat and she was burning all my clothes.

I fell back into an uneasy sleep and a sixth sense woke me up because there was Trudy standing over me with a big kitchen carving knife ready to plunge it into me **Argh !!** I wrestled the knife from her and threw her outside the door. I looked for clothes but she had burned them all except for a pair of red shorts of mine. I had no top to wear, Just a pair of bright red shorts and a pair of flip-flops but at least I had my wages. I tried to flag down a few taxi's but they just honked their horns and drove past until this taxi must have took pity on me and drove up and I said I'm having women trouble I showed him I had money and he had a spare top in his boot so I bought it off him and he drove me into Melbourne city. I waited then till the shops opened and bought a pair of long trousers as it was freezing and a cardigan and pair of shoes and had some breakfast and I thought bloody hell she would have killed me if I hadn't woke up. So the end of another romance for Danny boy, oh Lord I can sure pick them, eh.

I went to the Greyhound bar as I knew Charlie the other Glasgow brickie I was working with drank in there and when I met him I told him all that happened and he said you're lucky to be alive and I said don't I know it, so that was the end of Trudy and me. I got fixed up in the Diplomat hotel at St Kilda and stayed there for a few months, Charlie lived round the corner so he would pick me up in the morning for work in his car and working for this Joe Schmitt was OK. He had a block of flats to build and he said to us if I can get these flats built before the scheduled time I will give you all a bonus and take you for a weeks fishing trip on my boat. So we all worked like the hammers and finished the job well ahead of schedule and Joe was a man of his word, he gave us all a barbecue at this house on the last day of the job and paid us our wages and a good bonus. Only Charlie, Dennis the Yorkshire brickie and me Joined Joe for the weeks fishing trip, which was basically a jolly boys outing of non stop drinking. He did take us to the edge of the Pacific ocean and we stood there looking and as far as the eye could see it was a pure blue sheet of water as we stood on silver sand and I thought I will never forget this sight for as long as I live and I haven't.

Then Joe's work ran out and Charlie and me went working for another German subby called Peiter Leike. He gave his jobs out on price-work, he would run one site and a bricklayer called Dick Asquith from Essex ran the other site. I liked this guy Dick as he drank in the Greyhound bar which was now my local bar but I could not stand the boss at all, he was so big headed and conceited. I was working on Dick's job alongside Charlie, Kevin an Aussie brickie, then Ernest an Austrian brickie, Bernie a German Brickie, Langer an Austrian Brickie, Happy a Hungarian hoddie, Curly a German labourer and Charlie an Austrian Labourer an other league of nations and most of us got on well with each other.

In fact when I started working on Dick's job he said do you know anyone looking for accommodation, I have a flat at the back of my house and its vacant and I said yes that will do for me, so I moved into Dicks place and he drove to work each morning. When we got paid on a Friday this Peter Leike would meet us all in the Greyhound bar at 2.30 and pay us our wages in the back room of the pub. He would put his name down for a game of pool when he came in and when anybody from his "firm" played him they let him win everyone except me that is and I'm not the best pool player but not bad either and he hated it when I played him and wouldn't shake my hand when I beat him but I would shake his when he beat me. Although he paid good prices and I was saving money up big time but still drinking every night and there was a pub called the Village Bell nearby where I got my counter dinners. And then I would get a tram back to Dick's place.

In the Greyhound bar it was a very cosmopolitan mixture and everybody got on well with each other. I had a couple of Kiwi mates [New Zealanders] Richard and Ivan and they would be in there after work at night times, Richard was a roof tiler and Ivan was a mechanical digger driver. Anyway this night Richard had a right good drink in him and he couldn't start his car up to drive home until one of the lads started it for him and he said I'm passing your way Danny and I went with him, the good thing was that in Oz at that time it was compulsory to wear your seat belt so you automatically belted up soon as you got in the car, away we went and about a couple of miles we came to a set of traffic lights and the lights were just changing when Richard said to me what do I do and I said put your foot down and he did and we crashed right into another car and we both went spinning all over the place. When the cars stopped the other driver started his car up and drove off at ninety miles an hour, so I reckon he had drink driving too. If we hadn't all been wearing our seat belts who knows what. !!!

Then the following week Ivan said let me give you a lift home, he had been drinking but didn't look drunk so I accepted a lift home from him, no sooner had he got on the dual carriageway and he fell asleep at the driving wheel. I tried shouting at him to waken up but no good so what I did was grabbed the steering wheel and made us crash into the side of the road as he still had his foot on the accelerator. I finally got him to wake up but I said I'm getting a taxi Ivan let me give you a lift but he said he would sit till he sobered up then drive home so I left him and got a taxi back to Dick's place and every night after that I would drink in the Greyhound bar but would always order a taxi home, because you know what they say about third time lucky. !!

We happened to go to this Peiter Leikes job one day as Dick's job got held up, come lunch time and we all headed over to the pub and we were playing pool and everyone was letting this Pieter win, he "beat" everyone of our gang and I was last to play him and everyone knew I didn't like him. Just before our game of pool started Dick followed me into the toilet and said Danny for f**k's sake let him win. I went back out and it was down to a black ball game and this Pieter left the black right over the pocket I hit and pocketed the black but my white ball followed in after it. So he won by my default he was over the moon and we never went back to work staying there till 5 o'clock. Actually I did it on purpose as Dick had said to me in the toilet if he wins we can stay in the pub all day so for once I had "thrown" the game and everybody knew what I had done but ah sure what the hell we ended up having a good drink.

Time was flying in and Dick had started a new job all new flats and I liked working with him and our gang. Dick used to hold a barbecue in his back garden once every six weeks and people would come with one bottle of beer and expect to stay all day long Dick had a pool table in his garage so that would always be busy on barbecue days. Then when the drink had run out then all the hangers on would leave and I would bring out my beer which was in my fridge inside my place and we would drink till about midnight and the sing song would start and it was great. Most people when they came to Oz they wanted to make a new life for themselves which is fair enough but me I just treated it as a working holiday and one day at work I turned round to Dick and said I'm going back to South London to live and work and he was shocked but I had made my mind up as I missed all the pub life and music in Walworth and all my mates. I had been in Australia almost two years by this time and I had accumulated £4.000. Dick and his wife Linda and a few of my mates drove me to Melbourne airport and I was heading to Glasgow first of all to see my Ma and Da then it would be back down to South London.

Sitting on the plane the flight engineer came up to me and said would you move down a few seats mate, he said the side door I was sitting opposite hadn't closed properly and he started hitting the handle with a big wooden mallet to close it manually and I kept buzzing the stewardess for more whisky. I kept my eye on that door all the way back to Glasgow.

- - - - -

Chapter 12

West Germany 1st and 2nd Trips

So me and Maggie part company again and I go to West Germany to work for the first time. I had phoned up the telephone number in the Evening Standard newspaper and they said "go to Charing cross railway station and meet our Rep, Mr Fox and he will organise things from there" so that's what I did and when I got there there were about twenty bricklayers with tool bags and levels all standing there. I went over to this Mr Fox and he marked me down on his list. Then he bought all our rail tickets to Harwich [?] and we sailed over the North sea till we got to Holland and then decamped it was night time, so we were all billeted in a Hotel and in the morning after breakfast were taken by train to Nijmagen and it was here that there were loads of Volkswagen vans that took us all to different building sites in West Germany.

These Dutch subbys would say right four brickies for Dusseldorf or three brickies for Hamburg, etc. As fate would have it I was put together with another three bricklayers, John from North London, Richie from Wales and Eric from Ramsgate and we were driven by a Dutchman to a town called Celle which was about 40 kilometres from Hanover [and close to Belsen concentration camp]. the Dutchman drove us to our Hotel which was the Grunen eiche [green oak] and he introduced us to the owner Karl Heinz and his wife Margaretta who could both speak English which was a God send, two of us each to a room, we were shown to our rooms and they were nice and clean. We were told we could have breakfast and an evening meal which was great. Now the Dutchman said I will give you a sub off your wages on the second week of you being on site and at the end of the month you get all your wages minus the sub and that all seemed ok but I would rather have been paid weekly but if that was how it was then so be it.

The houses that we had to help build were about a seven minute walk from the Grunen eiche hotel so no buses to catch, on the first day we met the site foreman [Polei] and he held us all a shovel each, he couldn't speak English so that was a problem, anyway he with hand signals should us we had to dig the soft sand away to make a trench for the foundations of the new house. Normally we don't do that but when in Rome !!. We dug the foundations and then the concrete lorry pulled up and poured the concrete into the foundation, then we got the Architects blueprint to study and see what dimensions the brick foundations had to be. Luckily there had already been a few houses already built on the site so it was more or less just a copy. One of the carpenters on the job [called zimmermen] was called Bruno and he spoke perfect English so anytime we had problems we could go and talk to Bruno for help.

Now in Germany they are great beer drinkers and on this site [as all sites in Germany] you had a beer wagon that came every morning and sold small bottles of beer and cigarettes, so what the other German workers done was buy a couple of crates of these small bottles of beer and put them in the fridge supplied in one of the huts/sheds as it got really warm in Germany, then whenever you fancied a beer you sent someone to go fetch the beer. Although I have to say that the German workers would open up their small bottle of beer, take a swig and then they put a clip that fitted over the top of the bottle to stop the gas escaping but No not us as soon as we opened a bottle of beer it was "glug glug" and gone ha ha. You could have as many beers a day as you wanted as long as the work was going ahead. It seemed a friendly job and some of the Germans spoke good English, others couldn't so it was hand signals to them but we all got on well together.

When we had finished our first days work we were walking back to the Grunen eiche hotel and there was this Spar shop [mini supermarket] and on going in we just picked up chocolate bars or crisps and paid for them at the till with our German money [we had changed at the bureau de change] then Eric the lad from Ramsgate said I'd like milk so he said to the young lady assistant "milk" and she looked and shrugged her shoulders so Eric made a "moo" sound and made his fists go up and down as if he was milking a cow and she laughed and went to the back of the sop and brought back a pint of milk, see the hand signals do help. Lol. Then back to the hotel for a shower and our evening meal and of course a few beers to wash it all down with.

The local German people who drank in the Hotels bar were real good and tried to help us, some only spoke a little English but the others were pretty fluent so we got by, it was a Local custom when you passed by this big round table [stamp tish] where the locals always sat, you had to knock on the table with your knuckles and say guten morgan if it was morning time or guten tag if during the day and guten abend if it was evening time and they in return would answer back with the same. I was slowly very slowly picking up bits of the German language and when we sat down at the tables in the hotel it was waiter service so Herr Ober was the waiter and Frau/ Fraulein Kellereen was the waitress. Now the Germans are trusting people so when say four of us sat at the table and ordered four beers, then whoever ordered paid for them but all the waiter did was mark with his pen four 1111 's on your beer mat[called a declan] and put a stroke through the four 1111's which meant when you went home you handed your beer mat [declan] at the till to and they counted up haw many 1111's you had on your declan and paid the amount asked for, it saved keep going into your wallet all the time.

By the time we were into our second week at the hotel we were widely accepted as "das Englanders" although I was Scots and Richie was from Wales but it didn't worry me. John the brickie from North London and Richie from Wales were only in their very early twenty's where as I was almost twenty nine and Eric from Ramsgate was in his early forty's, Eric and me hit it off whereas I didn't hit off with the other two lads, just the way it

179

was, there were OK but not really my cup of tea. In Germany they drink schnapps and one night in the hotel I decided "to give it a go" and dear Lord was it strong, I was drinking steinhager schnapps and when you drink it you could feel it burning as it went down and then it "kicked in" with a warm glow over your face.

It seems quite a few of the local German people were sending me over a few glasses of this schnapps and I started to sing the old Elvis song "Wooden Heart" half in English and half in German and the locals absolutely loved it as I have always had a fair singing voice but I think it was the fact that I had sang a song that contained German in it that showed I was paying respect to the German people sitting there that made them love it and the schnapps flowed that night. Oh going to work the next morning my head was thumping and I got to our site and had one of the small bottles of beer straight away to try and clear my head. By this time it was the second week we had been there and the Dutchman came on the site and paid us a sub as he had promised, so that night we paid Karl Heinz the hotel owner our hotel and food/drink bill as we had more or less been on the "slate". he was happy and we were happy.

We continued working on that site and we were enjoying it we had now got the house with all its brickwork and internal blockwork up to the first floor joist level and the carpenters [zimmermen] came and laid the joists and we carried on building above it while drinking our bottles of beer while doing so, although we did have a tea break and lunch break in the huts but not a drop of tea was in sight it was just beer. Every now and then the architect would drive up in his Mercedes car and go to the boot of the car and bring out a crate of beer for the workers as the German belief is if you don't give the workers a drink they will make a bad job of the work.!!!. So all in all everything was going well until the end of the month and **total disaster** struck. The Dutchman drove on the site and went to the site agents office and got all our wages [in cash] and then drove off the site at a hundred miles per hour in a cloud of dust.!

We had all been knocked for our wages, we owed our hotel bill and food/drink, how could that Dutchman have done this to us, but he had and we were all totally gutted. Then fair play to the German site manager he said you are all good workers why don't you come and work for us directly and we said yes. We told Karl Heinz what had happened and he was raging over what the Dutchman had done but he said stay with us and when you get paid by the main contractor on site you can pay me then and we all thanked him sincerely. All the local German people were also disgusted and they rallied round to help us any way they could. We got paid once a month working directly for the German firm and by the time we had got our second monthly wage we had paid back Karl Heinz in full.

John and Richie the other two bricklayers said they had had enough and said they were going home which is fair enough as everyone must do as they see fit and so they went back to London and Wales respectfully. That just left Eric and me and because of that we were put to work with another gang of German bricklayers on site, there were seven of them, six brickies and one labourer and none of them could speak a word of English so it was all back to hand signals again,lol. Then another disaster because Eric fell off a scaffold and busted his ribs so he couldn't work poor lad and was confined to laying in his bed at the Grunen eiche, the only good thing was because we were working direct for the firm he got full pay but he was in agony and was off work for a month and inside that month I was thrown into the lions den and had to pick up the German language. I had already picked a fair bit of it but it was do or die and I have to say I think I done well, I started trying to read the German newspapers and got the locals back in the hotel to help me when I got stuck. By the time Eric came back to work I don't say I was a fluent German speaker but I could walk into a cafe/restaurant and order a meal from the menu and hold a basic conversation.

It was good to see Eric back at work but he told me he had personal trouble, he had remarried this lady called Ann who was now living back in Ramsgate in their house and she had a terrible first marriage to a bully and was very nervous and I though then why did he leave her and come to Germany to work but I never did. Cut a long story short he said to me if I bring Ann over would you like to share a flat with us and I said yes. So one weekend he went back to Ramsgate and brought his wife back to the Grunen eiche hotel where the local people made a big fuss over her as the locals all liked Eric and they helped Eric find a flat and cut a long story short the three of us moved into a flat in the town of Celle, Eric had bought a car so he drove us to work and back and at the weekends go for a drive but I went to the bars at the weekend and left Eric and Ann to be together.

I have to say she really was such a nervous person and I thought she was always ready to burst into tears. She stayed in the flat all day long while Eric and me were at work, there was a TV in the flat but the programmes were all in German so she was stuck indoors all day long reading a book which must have made her more depressed. Time marched on and it was now six months since I had been in Germany and Eric said Ann and I are going home for a weekend to Ramsgate. We will drive to Dover and then get the ferry over do you fancy coming and I said yes I can go up to London for the weekend and see some of my mates. We took Friday off of work and drove to Dover and when we got there we held our passports to passport control and the guy handed them all back to Eric who put them all in the glove compartment and said I'll keep yours in there too Danny and I said no probs.

Then I got the train up to London and was knocking on my big pal Richies door and he and his wife Beryl were glad to see me and they kindly put me up for the weekend until I traveled back down to Ramsgate to meet up with Eric and Ann and dive back to Germany. It was good being back in South London again and Richie and me went to a few of the pubs down East street and before I knew where we were it was Sunday morning, I thanked Richie and Beryl and got the train back down to Ramsgate. Eric had given me his home land-line number saying just ring that and we'll come pick you up. I did this but there was no answer so I gave it ten minutes and then rang again and again and again for over two hours it was quite clear to me that Ann was not going to go back to Germany and looks like she had persuaded Eric to stay at home. What could I do, luckily enough I just had enough money left for a train ticket back to London and was knocking on Richie's door again.

Fair play to Richie and Beryl once again they put me up and he gave me a few quid to tide me over, next morning I went back to that big barrier block job at Coldharbour lane in Brixton and the foreman bricklayer John Quinnliven started me straight away. I said John all my tools are over in Germany and he got me a loan of a few tools so fair play to him. I stayed with Richie and Beryl for a few nights and then on Friday night moved into digs in St Giles rd Camberwell. I did phone up Eric a month later, he said sorry and posted my passport back.

West Germany

2nd trip

My second trip to West Germany started the same way my first one did and the other bricklayers met Mr Fox at Charing cross railway station and it was the train to Harwich and the ferry over the North sea but this time and I don't know why we landed in Belgium and we stayed in a hostel until the following morning and we got the train through to Nijmigen in Holland and once again all the Dutch subbys were waiting in their Volkswagen vans to drive us to different building sites in West Germany. This time they wanted six brickies for a place called Mainz which was a fair sized town of two hundred thousand people [approx] and the nearest city to that was Frankfurt. Right so the Dutchman drops us off at our Hotel the Kleine Willheim [?] and its a Sunday evening and the first person I see sitting down having a drink is a friend of mine Patsy Lovell who was a foreman bricklayer for Dave Donnghue back in South London, yes sure is a small world.eh.

It works out its a Hypermarket we are building which will not only sell food but motor cars, cement mixers and everything else under the sun and when I see it the following morning its a massive sized site. I think there are twenty of us living at this hotel and Heidi is the manageress and I start to speak to her in German and she is over the moon as she can't speak English. So I end up like Dennis the bricklayer in Aufweidersehen Pet and become the go-between at the hotel. Heidi tells me that some lads have been taking liberties and she wants me to tell them she wants to chuck them out, so I sit down with everyone and tell them that Heidi is doing her nut and to be short and sweet either behave or get out. Well it must have worked as Heidi said "danke schoen mein freunde" [thank you very much my friend].

On the site I'm working in a gang of four bricklayers all good lads and we have this German foreman overseeing us, so I speak to him in German and we form a bond, hes not a bad guy but can't speak a word of English except hello and cheers, so he was having problems before trying to tell the lads what he wanted done and Now that I was there that solved a lot of problems for him. This site was so big that they had two permanent beer wagons on site and the firs thing in the morning was get a crate of beer put it on the scaffold and then go back and get the tools [we had to get our priorities right]. oh dear Lord we didn't half drink some beer all day long, I was now trying to pace myself otherwise I would have ended up singing "Wooden Heart" on the scaffold we were working on.

We actually have the use of two Volkswagen vans [although I can't drive] and sometimes the lads at the weekend nights would drive into the nearest town about 5 miles away for some night life although I usually stayed at the hotel and had a drink and would play cards or at the weekends have a sing song and I was always asked to sing [not being big headed but I had not a bad voice] and Heidi was always buying me a drink and every night I went upstairs to my bed I would say to her "Ich liebe dich"[I love you] and she would reply "Ich auch" [me too] but that's as far as it went.

We got paid weekly from this Dutchman and that was a change from getting paid monthly or worse getting knocked for your money and it was all in German bank notes. Some of the lads who came over to Germany to work wanted to save money up and send it home every week to their wives/family and there was nothing wrong with that at all but I think the majority of lads [including me] just used it as a working holiday and have a good drink while doing it. We started work at 6.30 am and finished at 6.30 at night, so you can imagine it was a long old day but the beer made it bearable and it was good money too, we worked Saturday till one o'clock and Sunday's off. So usually on a Saturday it was back in the vans to our hotel and shower and change and head off into town and I did this a few times with the lads to be sociable.

Although Sunday was a lazy day and one of the van drivers would drive into town and get a few newspapers but it would be Saturday's edition of the Mirror or whatever other British newspaper they had on sale and they were devoured for all the news. Then it would be an all day long drinking session in the hotel for most of us, sometimes a row would break out but I quickly stepped in and made sure the lads shook hands and said have a beer or wine and forget it, remember were all a long way from home. A few of us would play cribbage or whatever card game you liked just for a small amount of money to make it interesting. Then have something to eat in the hotel and have a kip and back down to the bar at night for more beer and perhaps a sing song and all of a sudden it was back on site for Monday morning and building bricks again.

Then we got the offer of doing some price-work on this Hypermarket and myself and another few lads took it, it was great big long brick walls and we couldn't help but make money and could still have a few beers on the scaffold but not as much as before when we weren't on price-work and I though

I could end up going back to South London with a nice few quid in my pocket. All in all life was OK on my second trip back to West Germany until one night it was a Friday night and we had all been paid in cash and some of the lads said you coming into town with us Danny and I said yes what the hell and off we piled into one of the Volkswagen vans, in fact the two vans went that night and we pulled up at this bar which was a bout five miles from our hotel.

We all piled into the bar about sixteen of us and we sat at the bar and ordered a beer and I must say I liked the German beer [schnapps was good but only once in a while] I'm sitting at the bar when this girl came and sat beside me and said will you buy me a drink and I did she ordered a "cognac" and swallowed it in seconds, of course I knew what was happening she was a "house girl" and every time she had a drink bought for her she got a "commission" and that wasn't "cognac" she was drinking it was probably cold tea. She then said will you buy me another and by this time she was rubbing my leg so I did buy her another drink which again was swallowed in seconds. Then she said to me would you like to go into the back room where we can be more comfortable and I said oh yes, or rather Ja, ja.

We left the bar to the cheers from all my workmates and we entered a back room which had little cubicles each with a pull around curtain and we sat in the first cubicle and we started to kiss and just at that moment the "Madame" of the place came in with a great big tray of these "cognacs" and placed them in front of the girl who started to drink them as fast as she could and I said to her "langsame" "langsame" which basically meant slow down. She did for a while and then said to me you look like a "Kleine Elvis" [small Elvis] I was young had a good head of hair, was nice and slim but only a slight resemblance to Elvis. Never the less I tried to kiss her again and then the "Madame" came back in with another great big tray of these "cognacs" and I shouted "Nein" "Nein" [no, no].

The "Madame" of the place said she wanted paying for all these "cognacs" and I said "Nicht bezhalen" [not paying] when all of a sudden these two big six feet four tall shaven headed monsters appeared and made it quite clear that if I didn't pay they were going to break my arms and legs. What could I do, they took my wallet with all my price-work wages in it and handed me back the empty wallet, then opened the fire exit and I was shoved out onto the street but in the back ground I heard the girl saying "Kleine Elvis" will you come back next week and see me. !!!

I wasn't allowed to get back into the bar and none of my mates knew what had happened to me, I had no money at all so I had to start the long five mile walk back to Heidi's hotel but I had to be philosophical about it at least it wasn't raining and once again I thought to myself , why does it always happen to me. I got back to Heidi's and went to bed and told all the lads the next day what had happened and they all laughed , mind you so did I what else could I do.

A week went by and I got my wages and thought I had been in West Germany for six months so now its time to go back to South London, get new digs, see my mates and start working of which I did. So it was Aufwiedersehen Deutchland and back to South London.

- - - - -

Chapter 13

Thames Television Euston, Then Dublin

My big pal Danny McLuskey told me he was working over at Thames Televison studios at Euston rd but he had been offered price-work and was going to take it,so did I want his job at Thames TV and I said yes I would. So I started there and it was an ongoing contract, I knew the site agent Peter McKinley and he was a sound person, basically it was a new studio that was getting built inside the existing building and there was only Peter the agent, George the carpenter, Robbie our labourer and Terry the electrician.

I would be paid £60 per shift [minus self employed tax] and I would be paid at the end of every month. I didn't have a bank account at that time so asked Gerry the Guvnor of the Albert arms pub and he said he would cash it for me no prob as I was his best customer and Peter Wall at the Whitehouse where I was living said he could wait till the end of the month For his rent so I decided to take the job, of course I told Mo my ex wife she would have to wait till the end of the month for her money that I gave to her for my children and she also said that was OK.

I started and the first thing we had to do was help George the carpenter put up all the shuttering form-work that the new concrete floor would sit on and we had to prop up all the shuttering with steel jacks. This was a giant size room probably about thirty feet high so what we were doing was putting a new concrete floor in the middle and on top of that would be the new TV studio. We done all the form-work, steel props in place then done all the steel fixing work and poured the concrete floor. It was a piece of cake really as the concrete lorry had a pump fixed to it, the concrete was poured and leveled off within four hours, we then changed our clothes into our "going home clothes" and went upstairs to the Thames TV bar which we were entitled to use as we worked there. The prices were very reasonable so many a night after work we found ourselves in there.

We were also allowed to use the canteen/cafeteria at lunch time and it was heavily subsidized and you got a lovely lunch of say steak, chips, peas, a sweet and tea or coffee for next to nothing and if we were not in the pub at lunch time we went to the cafeteria. I remember there was a complaints book there and the guy in front of me wrote in it the peas are a bit on the hard side !!! and I thought of all the times in my life on the building sites sitting in a cement shed eating a cheese roll and drinking a pint of milk but then again maybe that guy has it right and us in the building trade have it wrong.

I used to see Sarah Kennedy the TV presenter a few times when I was working in the building and she came over as a nice person, there were plenty of free tea/coffee machines which was brilliant. I remember one day I had to build a wall on one of the floors and said to my labourer Robbie those TV props are in the way of the new wall so we started to move them when all of a sudden I heard a shout **Stop**.

Jim the guy in charge of the scene movers came over to me and said that is our job and our job alone to move scenery props and My union will have this studio out on strike if you ever do that again. Oh I said its not Robbies fault as I told him to move it, so blame me. He said don't do it in future then and I said OK I wont now that you have told me. As it happens I got to know this Jim pretty well and he was OK and many a drink we had in the bar upstairs. Then one day the same thing happened again TV props were in the way of a wall I was going to build and so I went to see Jim to get his men to move it and he said Danny I have no men at this studio today, oh sure just move it yourself. !!.lol.

We worked seven days a week here at Thames TV but we had an easy schedule to keep up with so many a day we were in the pub all day long and got paid for it as we were ahead of the schedule but because I was working seven days a week I couldn't take my girls out on Saturday or Sunday, so after being there for about three months I said to Peter the agent I'm jacking it in and I did. Then two things happened I got a tax rebate of £1.300 which I gave to Mo and then I headed over to Dublin to work.

I caught a flight to Dublin and started working for a Dublin subby called Mark Reilly and a real good guy he was. His job was on the north side of Dublin and was a new housing estate, I got digs in a place called Santry which wasn't that far away. Mark put me working with a Dublin brickie called Decaln and as it happens he used to live in Walworth and drank in the Kings head pub at Walworth rd/Manor place he was pals with Tommy Kelly a Dublin painter who drank in the Kings head and who I knew personally, sure is a small world.!!.

Mark the subby gave us the brickwork on a price and we made good money every week, Mark made an arrangement with the nearest Allied Irish bank and when he paid us on Friday we walked to the bank and got our cheques cashed in there no problem. I was drinking in a pub called the Comet in Santry which was close to my digs and was a massive pub. Lots of table service and no matter how busy they were they never forgot what you ordered. In fact they reckon a Dublin trained barman/woman are the best in the World. I would usually have about seven pints of Guinness every night after work and would sleep like a baby and be looking for a breakfast when I woke up.

There were a couple of bricklaying gangs there and as I say it was all price-work there so everybody was happy. A funny thing did happen one day our site was raided by the social security backed up by the Gardai [Irish police] and as soon as the social security men came on the site a few of the brickies and labourers climbed over the perimeter walls and ran away at ninety miles an hour. Obviously they had been "signing on" at the social security office while getting paid here on this job. One of the social men came over to me and I held him my passport and he phoned up to check me out and I was OK and said thanks as he handed my passport back.

I was on this job for about six months and saved up a fair bit of money and then I thought right I've had a good time but it was now time to go back to south London and told Mark that I was leaving and Mark said he was sorry to see me go but if I was ever back in Dublin again then to give him a phone call.

I actually did a few years later after I had came down from working in Belfast. Its always good to keep contacts for work in the building trade.

- - - - -

Chapter 14

Working for Sean Flood

So I went to work for big Sean Flood [born in Ireland brought up in Liverpool] when I lived in the Whitehouse, him and his partner Geraldine had a flat right opposite the Albert arms pub and he would pick me and a few other brickies and hoddies in his big van and drop us off at whatever site or sites he had going. He actually worked for a guy called Dave Gear and he paid Sean £10 a day for every man he got to work. I think Sean would have had about 12 to 14 men so that was either £120 or £140 per day for him while us Bricklayers were on £50 a shift [after tax] so he was coining it in and good luck to him he was nice big man and a good bricklayer.

I was having a week off work on the beer and on the Friday night in the Albert arms I asked Sean for the start and he said start in the morning which was a Saturday, not many people start the working week on a Saturday is there, ha ha. This job was down in Staines [on the way to Heathrow] and it was a bit of fancy brickwork so that suited me and I was there for about two weeks but at that time I fell down the stairs in the Whitehouse and was off work for a few days until the swelling of my black eyes went down. Then when I started back on the Staines job people never recognised me at first as that fall had altered my facial appearance but I was never a vain person so it never worried me.

Then my next job with Sean after that was out at Chessington [very near to Chessington zoo] and it was on an industrial estate and we had a big factory unit to build, there were ten bricklayers on the job and it was all straight work in between brick piers. So Sean had me building all the face brickwork corners and the other bricklayers would fill in between the corners I had built. This was a massive industrial estate and there were already many factories built there and the guy who owned the whole of this estate was always on site. He was a multi millionaire and not a very nice person, he was walking round the site with the site agent this day and shouted to me I don't like those two bricks that you have built take them out, that's when I said who gives you the right to speak to me like I'm a dog, anyway I said I never built those bricks somebody else did, so do yourself a favour and never speak to me again you piece of s**t. He was shocked and said don't you know who I am and I said well if you don't know who you are how the f**k do I know who you are and the site agent laughed and said to the guy Danny is quite right you have no right to speak to him like that, this infuriated him and he stormed off but never spoke to me again as long as the job lasted.

Then I worked for Sean on a Catholic Church down at Redhill in Surrey it was really fancy brickwork as the walls of the Church were serpentine shaped [squigly like a snake] and not only that they were built leaning back at an angle of five degrees and so we had a special wooden template built that we could use to make sure our brickwork was true to the lean back of five degrees. Sean had about eight bricklayers on the site but him and me were the only ones who could handle this type of brickwork, so Sean put the other brickies building the straight forward brick walls and bell tower while me and him built the tricky stuff.

It was in the sommer months and as usual I was wearing shorts and one Monday morning we went to the site with me feeling very rough from all the drink I had drank over the weekend I had been sitting in Sean's van for the best part of an hour as that's how long it took to drive from the Elephant to get to the Church. We arrived on site at eight am and it was lashing down with rain and the forecast was rain all day so I knew we would be driving back to the Albert arms as this is where Sean lived and dropped us off. The canteen lady came in at half eight and started to cook breakfast for all the lads but all I could face was a cuppa tea and a bacon roll [which I could eat half of] as I was feeling rough with all the vodka and beer I had drank the previous night. We stayed on site till a quarter to ten and Sean said come on its not going to stop raining lets get back to London, Mick the site agent was standing outside his site office above the canteen and looked down at me and said this is not a day for the shorts Danny and I shouted back up it will be when we get to the Albert arms Mick and Sean and all the other lads let out a laugh. We were on the way back and I said to Sean stop at the first off licence so I can get a can of lager to try and stop the DT's I was going through and he did, I drank the can but it never made me feel better so as soon as we got into the Albert I had a large vodka and coke followed by another and within half an hour I was feeling "half normal" again. We done the session that day in the pub and I went back to the Whitehouse when the pub closed at three o'clock and half a kip till seven that night and went out at eight but only to have just a few pints so I would be OK for work in the morning and thankfully I was.

Then I worked on another couple of jobs for Sean and on the run up to Christmas he had another factory/warehouse to build at that big industrial estate at Chessington for that big mouthed multi millionare, I saw him but we never spoke. By that time it was Christmas week and we were finishing up work on the Friday, I went to work on the Monday OK but missed the rest of the week as it was cold mornings and to be truthful I had a drink in the Albert every day and even though I had run out of money I could go on the "slate" with Gerry and Katherine but always paying them back.

Come the Friday night and Sean paid me my one shift [Monday] and Sean had always told me never to be frightened to borrow money off him so I asked for a loan of £300 and he gave it to me no prob. I said take it off at £50. per week and after Christmas I never had a drink in six weeks, I paid Sean back his £300 and had almost a thousand pounds saved up [£50 notes under the carpet in my flat]. I was proud of myself and then "broke out" on the drink on the Friday night, I was in the

Elephant &Castle bar at the Elephant and Sean walked in and said well you done well Danny. On the Monday morning I turned up for work and Sean said I didn't think I would see you as you were drinking again and I said no Sean those days are over I'm not having Mondays off anymore but I had the rest of the week off on the beer. Ha ha, what am I like, but that's me a hard worker but prone to liking the beer.

Then I went to work for Sean over at west London at Acton it was a factory and there were two other brickies and two hoddies, it was only a smallish site so we had it finished in a month and that was the last time I ever worked for Sean, what a nice big man and a good bricklayer. He was a great laugh in the pub and he and Geraldine would be in the Albert arms at weekend nights when we had an "afters" he would be in good form singing and I would be singing too. Sean was almost twenty years older than me and as I write I'm 72 which would make Sean 92 so I wonder is he still alive? I certainly hope so.

- - - - -

Chapter 15

Sevenoaks and Tom Gleeson

I had worked for Tom Gleeson on many jobs over the years but this particular one was different from the other ones I had done for him it was a grade 2 listed building, it was an old barn [actually ancient] down in Sevenoaks Kent, a Canadian merchant banker had bought a mutli million pound house with a fantastic thatched roof and beside it was this run-down old barn which he bought. This super rich guy had a fantasy for Parrots and in his large garden he had nothing but parrot cages all over the place and with Parrots in them all, actually I shouldn't say this but his wife had a "beak" nose and maybe that's what attracted her to him ha ha.

The walls on this old barn were all twisted and the roof was too, so what we had to do was get the roof taken down by Tom's son in law Sean who was a carpenter and in charge of the job, take Polaroid photos first of all and then tag each separate roof rafter to know what position it would go back to after I had taken the old walls down. Sure most of the walls were missing as they had holes in them everywhere. They were old stonework walls so we had to clean the stones [order more] and my job was to rebuild them back the way they were which was all twisted. So once again we had to take Polaroid camera photos so we could double check as I was rebuilding them and round the windows it was all red brick arches, just flat arches and not segmental arches.

This was all down at the bottom end of the barn at the top end the architect had drawn up plans for a completely new face brick extension so all this was going to keep me busy. Sean would pick me up at the Elephant on the New Kent rd in the morning at seven am as I lived on the Heygate estate at that time and pick the other lads up in Peckham. We had a very small wooden shed on site where we had our tea break and kept the architects drawings. I had internal walls to build at the bottom end of the barn, concrete block cavity walls with steel mesh inserted in the cavity and filled up with concrete to make it a double strong wall and to hold back in place the earth which would be resting against it with part of the new extension sitting on top of this earth but obviously with a concrete floor. Personally I would just have built solid concrete block walls [high density blocks] but this is what the architect specified so who was I to argue?.

On the first day that Tom drove me down there in his van he took Peter one of his foremen and a good mate of mine [who also liked a drink] we were all in the front of Tom's pick up van, we entered a narrow street and halfway down we came to a pub called the Beehive [lovely thatched roof] and immediately opposite the pub was the turn up into the old barn but it really was a sharp incline. Its on this side of the Barn that the new extension would be built and the barn below. As we passed by the Beehive pub Peter and me exchanged glances and we both knew what each other was thinking.Lol. So we just had a look around that day and Tom went through the architects drawings with Peter and me although the job would be run by his son on law Sean.

First day proper on the job after Sean had picked us all up in his van and we got around to taking down all the roof rafters and placing them to the side with tagging each one and this took a couple of days alone, then it was my job of pulling down all the walls and cleaning the stones so I could rebuild them later. Then it was Friday and Tom had given Sean all our wage packets on the Thursday evening so we paid our first visit to the Beehive pub at lunch time and looks like we weren't made very welcome and the Guvnor behind the bar made it be known it was a nuisance having all this building work going on.!!

197

So as time goes by I'm rebuilding the stonework walls back up to their twisted shape and the architect said to Tom, "Danny is doing a good rough job" as this is the way he and the client wanted it. The client, the merchant banker came out a couple of times and we said good morning but he wasn't the nicest of people and his wife we said hello to as she was hanging washing out in the garden but got no answer [what's the matter with these people!!] Things are going well and I get all the stonework built and the red brick arches too, so its up to Sean to get the old roof rafters up and that took a lot of manhandling but he did a great job. I went to build the internal block cavity walls with mesh in it but as I went to build the first course the earth bank behind the wall gave way it was like an avalanche and I had only seconds to jump back bloody hell it gave me a fright.

Then one day Tom drove down to visit us and it had been raining and the streets all wet, anyway he drove up the steep incline to get onto the Barn job and his wheels kept slipping because of the rain and his van slid back down the hill and crashed into the Guvnor of the pubs car which was parked outside the pub. He came running out of the pub screaming and shouting but fair play to Tom he said I'm sorry but my insurance will cover any damage and use of a hired car, this calmed him down a bit but he was still fuming. So you can imagine the next Friday we popped in there for a Friday lunch drink the atmosphere was very cold to us.

Anyway we now were concentrating on building the extension to the barn at the top and first of all we had to get the concrete lorry in and we had to lay the extension floor. The only way the concrete lorry could get onto the barn's site was to reverse up the street from the bottom and reverse up the steep incline. So Sean had to get notes printed and post them through everybody's letter box giving them a few days notice to keep their cars away from the bottom end of the street to allow the concrete lorry to get up and again you can imagine this didn't make us too popular with the locals. But what happened next was unbelievable, the concrete lorry made it up to the barn OK and dumped all the concrete so we were busy leveling it when the concrete lorry driver said quick get behind the wall, one of the big tyre's on the truck was expanding at an incredible rate.

The driver said I have seen this happen once before and the tyre will explode like a bomb. !!. true to his word there was an almighty **Bang** and all you could hear was the tinkling of glass as surrounding windows shattered and the Guvnor of the pub came running out of the pub with a napkin tucked into the top of his shirt and a knife and fork in his hands [he was having lunch] he was screaming "first of all you smash my car up and now you are trying to blow us all up, well that's it you're all barred from my pub, you're barred do you hear" and we were all rolled up laughing behind the wall.

I then built all the brickwork on the barn extension and for me my part of building the barn was over but for Sean he had all the carpentry work to do and the electricians, plasterers, painters, etc would have work to do. Once again I had the wanderlust bite me and I decided to go back to Ireland to work, the architect Bernard thanked me for doing a good job and wished me good luck and then I shook hands with Tom Gleeson who said if you're ever back in London give me a call and with that I caught a flight to Belfast and would stay with friends of mine before starting work on the new Belfast Hilton hotel.

- - - - -

Chapter 16

Ireland Again

So I fly into Belfast and stay with friends of mine out in West Belfast on a housing estate called Poleglass, I had been over in Belfast on a good few occasions for St Patrick's day processions [as I did in Dublin and New York] and being of Irish descent I was always sympathetic to the National cause for reunification and played a small part in that, over the years terrible things have been done to all sides by all sides including both the Irish and British governments but now we have a political process in place and although bitter pills must be swallowed its the only ahead. Oh yes I'm still for a united Ireland but if not then I would settle for a united people. Politics alone are the way forward and no more violence.

So I stay with my friends Ciaran and Delia and after being there for a week I start work on the construction of the new Belfast Hilton hotel at the markets area of the city and there are about fourteen bricklayers there and I must say it was an interesting job, plenty of face brickwork with a bit of stone work here and there. I get the bus into the city centre every morning and its only a five minute walk from there to the site. I'm working alongside an older bricklayer called Billy, he's a good brickie but a bloomin moaner so after a while I get a transfer to work with another brickie called Doc and he's a great lad to work with. There is a fair bit of radius [circular] brickwork and I like this type of work as its out of the ordinary.

We have a foreman bricklayer on the job called Jackie and he's a good guy but the main man was Edgar the Clerk of works and he was a nice man, he spoke to everyone and addressed them by their first names but was no fool he wanted a first class job done and wouldn't suffer those who couldn't do it. We got on very well and lots of times he would get me to build "special works" and said to me when this job is nearing its end you will be the last bricklayer on it, you'll be coming in dressed in your slippers and titivating work here and there when the carpets are all laid down. Which was a very nice compliment indeed.

The Guy I worked for was called Kieran O'Hara who was a bit of a fly boy, some bricklayers would be short in their wages come a Friday but I have to say my wages were always spot on. I remember the first Friday I was there our lunch break was at one o'clock and we came out just after half one, anyway we were building bricks and at twenty five past two all the brickies started cleaning their trowels and I said to Doc "what's happening" he said "we finish at half two on Fridays" I said "why" and Doc said "because everybody in Belfast likes a drink" well that suited me and this Kieran O' Hara turned up and paid us our wages all in cash and I went to the pub with some of the lads.

After being at Ciaran and Delia's place at Poleglass I moved into digs on the Falls rd because it was nice of my friends to put me up but they needed their own space as I needed mine. There were a couple of pubs nearby so after work finished I would get the bus to my part of the Falls rd and have a drink in the local pubs then there was a Chinese take away or a fish n chip shop where I could buy my evening meal or go back to my digs and cook a meal as I had use of the kitchen in my digs.

Belfast is a lovely town but sadly there was a divide there and you could only use certain pubs and I knew where to go to and where not to, again which was sad. The pub opposite to where I lived was called the Beehive and it had live music on there at the weekend so I would usually be in the music lounge Friday or Saturday nights. Overall I was having a good time in Belfast when the wanderlust took over again. I had been in Belfast for over six months and decided to go back down to Dublin to live and work and yes Danny boy was on his way again.

Dublin

I landed in Dublin and went to live with friends of mine in Clondalkin South Dublin, Denis and Mary and in the pub they drank in a builder was looking for a bricklayer so I went to build an extension to a house out beside Leopardstown race track and was finished in two weeks so I phoned up Mark Reilly the subby I had worked for before when I was in Dublin and he started me straight away at a place called Tallaght and in fact I got digs out at Tallaght. I moved into a room in a three bed-roomed house owned by a guy called Gerry Bailey who was a Disc Jockey, the other room was let out to a guy called Neil who was a barman in one of the Tallaght pubs. This suited me as I had the run of the house till gone midnight and could sit and watch TV on my own knowing the other lads wouldn't be in till much later. I started work for Mark Reilly at this big housing estate in Tallaght, I didn't have a labourer so I put a mix in the cement mixer myself and got the fork lift driver to drop it next to the wall I was building. I was building a great big long boundary wall so the blocks were all in pallets and dropped off beside the wall and I just loaded the blocks from the pallet and put them close to my wall. It was hard work being on my own so Mark gave me another brickie called Tommy and we would take turns in putting a mix in the mixer but this Tommy wasn't a good bricklayer so I went back working on my own and still made fair money.

Some days I would load out hundreds of blocks for about three hours and then put a mix on, there were about four gangs of bricklayers all using the one mix so I would wait till tea time when no one was near the mixer then put a couple of quick mixes on and give the fork lift driver a "drink" to quickly drop my cement mixes to me and my wall. Things were going well and Mark had made an arrangement with the local bank to cash our cheques up and one of the other brickies gave me a lift in his car at lunch time for the bank. Then Mark said to me I have a big housing estate starting in county Kildare and I can give you Kelly a hoddie who is trying to become a bricklayer and he has a car and lives not far from you, so I said why not.

I hit off straight away with Kelly and we get a new labourer to assist us and that way Kelly can lay blocks and bricks all the time with Ray our now Hoddie looking after us. It only took us a half hour to get to the site at Kildare by car and it was a nice job which was going to be built in three phases. I have to say though it seemed to be all blocks and some of them were heavy that we built on the houses with just a bit of face brickwork at the front of these houses and it seemed every time I looked up another big lorry full of concrete blocks would be pulling up and my back wasn't the best as I was nearing my 50th birthday and after a lifetime of building bricks/blocks I was suffering from wear and tear but I soldiered on.

I'm afraid my love life was nearly non existant at this time although I always had the option of visiting the massage parlours if I felt that way inclined. Usually when Kelly dropped me off at night time I would use Molloys pub in the centre of Tallaght and this was a huge pub that could easily hold over two hundred people with space left over. They also served meals and I had my eye on one of the barmaids there called Frances and I was just going to ask her out when she said to me I've just started going out with a new boyfriend can you get him a job, dash it I left it too late again anyway I got him a start with Mark Reilly and he wasn't a bad lad.

I loved drinking the Guinness in Dublin, it really was like drinking black coffee and there were two barmen standing in this Molloys pub and their only job was to keep filling up pint glasses of Guinness [well three quarters full and leave to settle] as the demand for Guinness was phenomenal. It was just one story high houses we were building on this Kildare job and they were flying up. The fork lift driver John was brilliant on this site he knew exactly what the different gang of brickies needed at the exact moment, be it more concrete blocks, bricks or window sills or lintels and he was well worth a "dropsy" come Friday.

I remember one day Kelly and me [Kelly was becoming a good bricklayer by now] with our hoddie Ray had worked hard, we were on the top lift of the house and we got all of the outside block-work all the way up to scaffold height and put the small scaffold up and built the block-work up to its finished roof height, all of this in one day. The Mortar was delivered on site in heavy duty plastic tubs and had a 48 hour retarder in it. John the fork lift driver just put the tubs where we wanted them. Anyway we drove home that night delighted we had done so much work that day but come the next morning which was a Friday it was like something from a horror movie, That night it had rained non stop and the rain had washed out all the mortar joints [remember 48 hour before the mortar sets] when we looked up at where our walls should have been it was just a mess of all the blocks laying on top of each other, everything we had built had fallen down with the rain. So Kelly and me said to Ray we will pay you the shift if you clean up all the blocks so we can rebuild them again and Kelly and me drove back to Tallaght and waited on Molloys pub opening . Sure these things happen.

Now my back was really playing me up with all these heavy concrete blocks and I had been back in Ireland for a bit over two years by now . So I thought Danny boy its time to get back to South London and start building the much lighter face bricks so I said goodbye to Kelly and Ray and the other brickies and once again said goodbye to Mark Reilly who reminded me anytime you're back in Dublin give me a call Danny and that was me on my way back to South London once again.

- - - - -

204

Chapter 17

Tony Carr

I first started work with Tony over at Shadwell In the East end of London it was my mate Bud O'Donnell also a bricklayer who said Tony's looking for brickies and he's paying good money [£140 per shift] so start I did but I made a "faux pas" on the first morning, see I saw the tower crane of the job and went inside the site, saw the site agent and said I'm a new start and he said then I'll induct you of which he did and after twenty minutes when the induction was over he said you can go upstairs to the canteen and have a cuppa tea before you start. I got in the canteen and quite a few men were there but not my mate Bud. Then my mobile went off and Bud said where are you and I said I'm sitting in the canteen, he said your on the site next door !! and so I was so I went next door and Bud Introduced me to Tony and the other lads and I started work and it was a block of flats that Tony and his works partner Brian Fox had taken from Paddy Doherty [The Pig] Paddy had three blocks on the site and had give this one to Tony and Brian at minus 20% of his prices.

It was all face bricks on the front and lightweight concrete blocks inside and was a three storey high block, only Tony, Brian, Bud, me and a young bricklayer called Chris and two hoddies Ron and young Andy, it was a happy "feel good"job and Tony was a character and great for a laugh. Like me he liked the 60's music and had a radio that was always tuned into Gold radio playing the old hits and we would have guess who the singer was just for a laugh which all made the time go in quick. Then all of a sudden we caught up with the concrete men who were doing the floors and Tony transferred us all out to another of his jobs out at Northolt which was a bit of a jaunt to get to and when we got off the tube station at Northolt it was a fifteen minute walk to the site but I decided to stick it out. Tony was a laugh as I said but his partner Brian was a bit gloomy, oh a real good bricklayer but I wouldn't go out for a drink with him.

[Photo above is Tony Carr extreme right, my hoddie Micky Doherty in the middle, and me to the left, that's my vodka in front of me.lol]

So we were on this job at Northolt and Brian had to go somewhere for a week and I was setting out brickwork for Tony and he said to me how would you like to be foreman bricklayer for me and I said OK I'll give it a go. He had a big job coming off at Bow, in fact he had one job at Bow which he took off the Pig at a 20% less off his prices but this other job at Bow he got the prices direct from the main contractor and this was the one he wanted me to run. It was eight story high flats mainly block-work but with a bit of face brickwork. The job was a bit of hit and miss because on some floors the steel work wasn't finished so we had to leave half finished work and go up to the next floor etc and I had to get some blocks cut down to a certain size in readiness for my bricklayers to build but lots of the labourers working for the main contractor were Polish and couldn't speak English and would chuck all these special cut blocks into the skips breaking them. This was after I had left messages on top of them saying "do not touch"!! I had to get an English speaking Polish lad to try and tell them not to touch them but they just carried on doing it.

Plus Brian was walking round the site when he visited it and was asking the bricklayers questions, that's when I said Brian I am the foreman bricklayer if you have any questions to ask then come ask me and don't undermine my authority. He said yes but I found out he was still doing it so I jacked up and left Tony and went working for someone else. I went back to the site on the Friday to get my money and it was all there and Brian said you can have a job with us for years to come but he didn't seem to realise it was on a point of principle that I had jacked over.

Anyway I had been away for six months and Tony asked me to go to his other job at Bow [The Pigs job] and I did and he had two blocks of flats to build and it was OK but some heavy concrete blocks so I said to Tony keep me on the face bricks otherwise I'm off and fair play to Tony he did. Then he got another great big site to build over at Bow and he asked me to run it and I said I will but no interference from Brian, so off I went and the site agent Liked it when I was running the site. Brian Fox would be on the job too a lot of times, so it was like he was running part of it and I was running the other part of it. Tony Pendry the site agent said can't you get Brian off the job to another job and I said I wished I could.

So Brian Fox and Tony Carr go to do work elsewhere and its just me running the job and Tony the site agent says "oh thank God the job runs so much smoother when you're in charge Danny" and for three months all is going well and one day in the summertime the bricklayers are all building this large gable end face brick wall but the sun is shining off the silver insulation boards in the cavity and its blinding the brickies so at four o'clock one comes down to me and says I have a splitting sore head with the reflection of the sun and so I go up to the gable end wall and the other brickies are saying the same so I said "right it's four o'clock now I will send you all home and pay you to five o'clock but tomorrow when its cool in the morning I want you all to work a bit faster and that will make up for that hour" and said does "everyone agree and all said yes".

Next morning at tea time Brian comes on the job and hes asking all the bricklayers what time did they finish last night [somebody must have phoned up either Tony or Brian] I found out and when I did I put my tools in my bag and with my level in my other hand walked off the site but told Tony Pendry the site agent why I was going. I went back to the site on Friday to pick up my wages and Brian had them ready and I said I told you before Brian that anytime you have questions to ask about a job that I'm running then you come and see me and don't ask other people. He took a red face and just walked away and I left to go and work elsewhere.

Then I think it was a bout a year later that Tony Carr phoned me up and said you working and I wasn't at the time, he said I have a house to build out at South Ruislip and I said its too far away, he said its only two weeks work then I have a job at Wimbledon which was a straight run on the tube so I said Ok. We went to build this house at Ruislip and the foreman on the job was Paddy a chippy. We quickly built the block work up to first floor joist level and built the face bricks in front of them. Then we built in the metal joist hangers in and built the block work to roof level.

As we were building the face bricks on the front again Paddy said next time you build in joist hangers make sure you have the right measurements, anyway I said it was me who measured them Paddy so let me go and check them and the measurements and joist hangers were all OK. Paddy wouldn't let it go and kept mumbling under his breathe and Tony was getting uptight until he snapped and ran down the ladder and all of a sudden Paddy and Tony are punching each other and the neighbours are out all watching this when the main builder dives up in his car and gets out shouting Stop, Stop. Anyway Tony and Paddy shook hands said sorry and actually became mates. I wonder what the neighbours thought, eh.

So we get down to the Wimbledon job and its a disaster of a job and I and I said Tony this job is not for me mate and said I'll see you for my money on Friday. When I got back to the Elephant my mobile phone went it was Brian Fox and he said Danny we have a load of garden/boundary walls to build at the Shadwell job, it will only be you another brickie and a hoddie and I said OK because I don't like holding grudges. So I started working there and was there for a few months and then Tony's work dried up so I left.

Tony did get another small job it was a bit of work for Tony Pendry [site agent at Bow] and it was only a weeks work but it was handy enough. Tony Pendry said he was going to break out on his own and wanted me to be his foreman bricklayer as I was old school and he would pay me well with bonus's every six months but it couldn't have worked out as he never phoned. Now that was a pity.

Of course the next time I worked for Tony Carr would be the last time, that would be for his job out at South Croydon and unbeknown to me that would my last job before I was thrown on the scrapheap at the age of 61 with that terrible recession and the arthritis in my knees and hands making it impossible to carry on working.

- - - - -

Miscellaneous Chapter

Bits and Pieces

Walworth

Walworth is a district of south London, England, within the London borough of Southwark . It adjoins Camberwell to the south and Elephant and Castle to the north, and is 1.9 miles (3.1 km) south-east of Charing Cross. Major streets in Walworth include the Old Kent rd, New Kent rd and Walworth rd .

History

The name Walworth is probably derived from Old English Wealh "Briton" and the suffix -worth "homestead" or "enclosure" and, thus, "British farm".

Walworth appears in the Domesday book of 1086 as Waleorde. It was held by Bainiard from Archbishop Lanfranc of Canterbury. Its domesday assets were: 3½ hides; one church, four ploughs, 8 acres (32,000 m2) of meadow It rendered £3.

John Smith House is on Walworth Road, and was renamed in memory of John Smith , who was leader of the labour party from 1992 up to his sudden death in 1994. A former headquarters of the Labour Party, it was often seen in news reports at election times and in the background as people came and went from meetings of the Labour Party National Executive Committee. It was used by the London borough of Southwark as the home for its education department and reopened in July 2012 as a hostel.

St Peters Church, Walworth, built circa 1825, is an excellent example of the neo-classical style of church built by Sir John Soane. It is an indication of the wealth of the middle-class merchants who then lived in the vicinity that they could afford an architect of such prominence. Charles Upfold was born at Walworth Common and baptised at St. Peters. The church is home to the Monkey Gardens - which was once home to a menagerie kept by a past Reverend of the Church, but is now a garden.

Manor place baths is a former wash house in Manor Place off Walworth Road. It is a grade II listed building. The building was renovated by Kagyu Samye Dzong Tibetan Bhuddist centre who obtained a five-year lease in 2005. They opened it as their London centre, called Manor Place Samye Dzong on 17 March 2007. Adjacent is the Council's old recycling depot which is now closed and has been replaced by a new facility at 43 Devon Street, off Old Kent Road.

Walworth is also home to the Pullens buildings - a mixture of Victorian live/work spaces and yards. Many of the flats are 1 bedroom, and some of the flats still connect to the Workshops of any of the three yards (Illife Yard, Peacock Yard and one other). They all share communal roof terraces with extensive views over to the West End.

Walworth also used to have a zoo, in Royal Surrey gardens, which was visited by Queen Victoria.East street market is a major street market.. There are plenty of parks in the area, including:

Michael Faraday Park
Salisbury Row Park
Nursery Row Park
Burgess Park
Victory Park.

Walworth is made up of three wards - East Walworth, Newington and Faraday. All of the nine councillors for Walworth, are from the Labour party.

Regeneration

Large amounts of regeneration and gentrification are occurring in Walworth, including the proposed demolition of the Elephant and Castle Shopping Centre, the newly built Strata tower, the demolition and regeneration of the Heygate and Aylesbury estates, and redevelopment of St Mary's Churchyard as a new park. The Bakerloo line extension is planned to complete in 2028/29; two new stations are being built for it along Old Kent Road.

Mentions in Culture

The district of Walworth features in Charles Dickens' *Great Expectations*. Mr Wemmick resides here in a small wooden cottage.

Walworth is featured in the 2016 novel by Stella Duffy, London Lies Beneath, set in 1912 It is also featured in the 2017 film The Foreigner, as the restaurant of the protagonist Ngoc Minh Quan is based in this district.

Notable Residents

William Booth, founder of The Salvation Army,
     1 Kennington Row, Kennington Common.
Robert Browning
Sir Charlie Chaplin, born 1889, actor and director
Sir Michael Caine, actor
Alan Ford, actor, born here in 1938
John Ruskin
Charles Upfold
Charles Babbage

Bill Bailey

Walworth Jumpers

Michel Faraday

Samuel Palmer

Frank Stubbs,, recipient of the Victoria cross,
    born December 3, 1888.

- - - - -

Chatham Street

When I was building bricks on the Salisbury estate in 1977 Patsy Patton the general builder was refurbishing the houses/flats in Chatham st and in the middle there was spare ground where Patsy used to have his building sand delivered and bricks and blocks too. In fact he built gates there to keep thieves out. He actually built his office and workshop there at a later date and kept lorrys and machinery in there so he actually "squatted on this spare ground" and in time to come this is where lots of his men would meet at 7.30 in the morning to be driven to his various sites and I know as I was one of them.

Patsy liked a drink as most [but not all] of us in the building trade do but back in the late 70s/early 80s Patsy would go "missing" for a week or two and his sidekick would get the men a sub on Friday but I must stress that as soon as Patsy appeared again every man got exactly what was owed to him, I have never ever known Patsy to "knock" anyone for money he's too good a man for that.

I knew some of the bricklayers who worked on the refurbishment of Chatham st back in the late 70s who were Joe Murphy, Dennis Dooley, Paddy Marks etc and I worked with them all on various sites throughout South London over the years. In fact Paddy Marks took control of the brickwork anytime Patsy went "missing" and like me was saddened when Paddy passed away.

Now the "funny" thing was that over the years because Patsy had "squatted" on the spare ground at Chatham st I think it actually became his property and a few years ago he sold it to property developers who built lots of flats there. Remember when you look at the photo below there is a gate that residents who have flats at the back use to drive in and park their vehicles. If what I'm told is correct then Patsy must have made a "bomb" selling this spare ground. Talk about the luck of the Irish.!!! Lol.

[Photo above shows where the new flats that were built in Chatham st in between the two white bay windows, and to the very left you can see the drive in gates for people who live in the flats inside at the back of the driveway]

I Worked for Patsy Patton over the years and he was a good man to work for and I have nothing but the highest respect for him to have given the drink up which must be hard as I don't think I could ever do that. If Patsy owes anybody money he always carry's their wage packet in his pocket until he meets them.

214

I never once had a falling out with Patsy but I did with his side-kick who was Patsy Russell and a couple of times I left the firm because of this Russell, who to me just didn't know how to speak to men properly but that's all water under the bridge now.

- - - - -

Taxi for Mr Gill

In the late 1980s when I was living and sharing a flat with my big pal Danny McCluskey over at Bayswater/Paddington [before I moved back onto the Heygate estate] I would still use the Albert arms pub at Garden row but I also used the Duke of Clarence at st Georges Circus which was only a stones throw away. One Saturday night I was in the Clarence and I had a fair drink in me, I was up dancing with some lady when the Landlady Edna said Danny I have ordered a taxi for you and I got a bit "stroppy" and said when I want a taxi then I'll order a taxi myself.

[Photo above is of the Duke of Clarence pub where a taxi was ordered for me.]

So I stormed off from the pub in a bad mood and walked or staggered down London rd to the Bakerloo line tube station at the Elephant&Castle intent on getting the tube to Paddington and changing over to the district line to get to Bayswater and back to my flat. Unfortunately it didn't work out that way.

Because I fell fast asleep and somebody gave me a shake and said it's the end of the line mate **What !!** I had only not passed by Paddington tube station but had now landed at Harrow and Wealdstone tube station which was the very last stop. Oh I could have kicked myself but then I heard one of the tube workers shouting out last tube back to central London leaves in one minute, so I quickly got up and ran up and over the footbridge and just made it into the tube before the door closed and I thought right I must stay awake and get off at Padding tube station.

I'm afraid I never did and where did I wake up, yes back at the Elephant&Castle tube station and once again. I could have kicked myself [see that drink has a lot to answer for ,eh] so what did I do.

I walked along London rd and completely sober now back to the Duke of Clarence pub and I knew they were having an "afters" because I could hear peoples voices, so I knocked on the window and Edna the Guvnor's wife drew back the curtain and I motioned with my hand for a drink and she shook her head and closed the curtain.

So I then had to look for a taxi but just couldn't get one so I ended up walking all the way back to Bayswater which took me we about an hour and half and I was definitely stone cold sober by the time I reached my flat.

So the moral to my story is next time a taxi is called for you take it otherwise you might live to regret it.

- - - - -

216

East Street Market

I will always remember the first time I saw East street market which was back in 1969 as a young 21 year old and fell in love with it straight away, all the barrows/stalls stretching for as far as the eye could see, the owners shouting out their wares and the buzz of the throngs of people and all the bargains to be had.

There has always been something magic about the Lane to me although I have to be truthful and say that it has changed since I first set eyes on it. Gone it seems are the traditional Cockney families who passed the stalls down to their families over the years. Now it seems the market is of a multi cultured mix and that is fair enough as we all have to mix with what is the meting pot of different nationality's and cultures and I'm not meaning to be disrespectful to any culture or creed as we all have the right to live and work wherever but I preferred it the way it was when I first saw it.

How I used to love taking my daughters when they were little girls down the lane on a Sunday morning and us all having a glass of sarsaparilla hot or cold. I still like the lane but to me its not the same as it used to be, I suppose its called progress.

[Photo above to the left is Dawes st 1940/50s ? and photo to the right is 4 East st traders.]

*[Photo top is East st traders enjoying a drink,
bottom photo is of East st tin sheds.
Full credit and many thanks to Darren Lock for all the photos]*

I wonder in years to come will East st market still exist ? as it looks like from the Elephant upwards we are going to have another regeneration of new buildings with people [with money] who can afford to live there are taking over from the previous traditional Cockney generations who were all brought up there. In fact it seems lots of Walworth born n bred people have already moved farther afield to various places and areas but at least we still have photos and out memories to look back on.

- - - - -

Malcolm Tyler

Once when I worked with Tom Gleeson [previously mentioned] he "loaned" me out to a builder called Malcolm Tyler who was from the Catford area of South London. I had to build a two story house at the back of Perry hill for him. It was all block-work with just a bit of face brickwork at the front of the house. Malcolm was/is a terrific guy and a great family man. Anyway Malcolm has two sons Andy and Jason, Andy being an electrician and Jason a carpenter and they all helped their dad with this job and I got on with them tremendously well.

Then when I was working with some other subbys I would get the call from either Malcolm or Jason and go and build other new houses for them and come Friday nights Malcolm would sign a cheque there and then and that was me paid up to that night [just like how it used to be in the old days]. Of course sometimes if I was working as foreman bricklayer for some outfit then I couldn't leave so I would go at weekends and build them extensions or whatever and that was with Jason who would labour to me and all went well.

I did quite a lot of work for Malcolm over the years and had the pleasure of meeting his lovely wife Chris and daughter Angela who married Dave an electrician he also like me was a Scot. Then Malcolm and Chris decided to move down to Poole in Dorset and asked me down to do brickwork/block-work on the house he moved into and I surely did as I have great time for Malcolm. In fact he asked me down to do more work for him, and his daughter Angela and Dave moved into a house in the same street that Malcolm lived in so once again I was getting the train from Waterloo station with my tool bag and level to do work for the family.

It was great working down in Poole and I also done a bit of work on his son Andy's house, Andy and Vanessa lived in a great big house and they wanted a bit of work done so I was their man. Then over the years I retired but Malcolm when he was up in London always met me in a Wetherspoons pub, bought me a drink and always slipped me a good few quid. Malcolm never forgot that I had came down to Poole to help do work for him and his family and I appreciated that deeply.

[Photo of Malcolm, his wife Chris and all their grandchildren.]

As I say I had retired but still saw Malcolm every now and then when he was up in London to look after his properties, then when I had been retired for six years [aged 68 then] he said to me fancy coming out of retirement !! I nearly had a heart-attack but I said yes, it was a days work about three hundred face bricks, which was a couple of brick piers at a window and a catnic [metal] lintel over the windows and build bricks over the lintels to the finished height. I knew I would never lose my skills but my speed was a bit on the slow side. Anyway I started at 8 am and finished at 5 pm but by this time my legs were shaking with not having worked for six years as you could imagine.

Malcolm thanked me and also said his daughter Angela was holding her 40th birthday party down in Poole and invited me down, he paid my return rail ticket and my hotel bill for my stay, hows that for generosity.!!!. in fact Malcolm paid for me to come to family events in Poole always buying my return rail tickets and hotel bill and I will never forget his acts of kindness to me or the family's.

He did phone me up about six months after I had done that days work for him and this time it was for about two and half hours work [about sixty face bricks and a bit of block-work] and that was the final day I ever built a brick because now the arthritis in my knees and hands kill me and now I have to use a walking stick to get about but I will never ever forget the kindness showed to me by Malcolm and his family.

Hopefully one day when this covid-19 virus is over or at least we have a vaccine for it I can meet up with Malcolm for a beer again. Many thanks to him and his family.

- - - - -

The Great Storm

It happened way back in 1987 and I was working for Sean Flood at the time and he dropped us off in his van after work at the Elephant next to the Albert arms pub, it was a Thursday night and even though I was living in a flat over at Bayswater I still liked having a drink in the Albert and then get a taxi back to my flat. That night was no different and Sean came in for a drink with some of the other brickies. It was always a good laugh in the Albert and I was also talking to some of my old pals who were still living in the Whitehouse.

Well that night and I'm not sure why but I was drinking rum and black and pints of Guinness [a good combination] and I swallowed quite a few of them, then about half eight I ordered a cab to take me back to Bayswater and when I got off there I went in to the pub I used there and continued drinking rums and pints of Guinness and stayed till closing time which was eleven o'clock.

I made my way back to the flat I was sharing with big Danny McCluskey but I think he must have been in bed and to be truthful I went to my bed too as I was half-cut, anyway the rum and Guinness sure knocked me out because next thing my alarm clock set for six am was ringing and groggily I reached over and turned it off.

Oh I must have a drink of water which I did then turned the electric kettle on to make a cuppa but the kettle didn't work and I thought hat's funny, so I went over and turned the TV set on to catch the morning news and the TV set wasn't working either and neither was the electric light so I imagined it was a power cut, so I drank more water and made my way to the tube station to start my journey to work.

When I left my flat I couldn't believe it trees were crashed over the top of cars and some other trees were uprooted and it looks like some brick walls had been knocked over and I thought what the bloody hell has happened. !!!. Anyway I walked to the tube station and saw more carnage every where I looked. I got to the tube station and it was closed ? and some people were standing outside and said its because of the storm last night. I thought what storm ?

So I walked back to my flat and when I got there big Danny was up and he said there had been a terrible storm last night but I had completely slept right through it thanks to the rum and Guinness.

At least the landline phone was working so I phoned up Sean Flood to say I couldn't get to work and he said Danny there won't be any work today because nobody will be able to get tubes, trains etc. He said I will have your wages ready if you can manage to get over to the Elephant today[as it was Friday pay day] so I took a slow walk through Hyde park and got to the Elephant at eleven am just as the Albert arms pub doors were opening and five minutes later Sean walked in with my wage packet. I told him I had slept right through this storm and he said it was really bad.

Anyway I was having a few pints of Guinness which made me feel better and by lunch time a few of Sean's other brickies and hoddies came in for their wages and we all ended up having a good drinking session and at closing time of three o'clock I ordered a mini cab back to Bayswater and stayed in Bayswater all weekend [although I had earlier phoned Mo who drove round to the pub and I gave her, her money for my girls].

So it was back to work on the Monday morning but the great storm of 87 had cause havoc all over the country and it gave plenty of work to builders all up and down the country, in fact a few years later I would rebuild walls that had been knocked over in the storm.

But when anyone says to me do you remember the great storm of 1987 I have to be truthful and so no I slept through it all, and not many people can say that. Lol.

- - - - -

The **Elephant and Castle** is an area around a major road junction in southeast London, England, in the London Borough of Southwark. Although the name also informally refers to the areas of Walworth and Newington, the proximity of the London underground station of the same name has led to the area being more commonly known as "Elephant and Castle". The name is derived from a local coaching inn.

"The Elephant", as locally abbreviated, consists of major traffic junctions connected by a short road called Elephant and Castle, part of the A3 Between these junctions, on the eastern side, is the Elephant and Castle Shopping Centre, with the Hannibal house office block above. To the north of this, bounded by Newington causeway and New Kent rd is the Metro central heights. The Strata residential block lies just south of the shopping centre on Walworth rd .

223

Traffic runs to and from the south-east of England along the A2 [New Kent rd and Old Kent rd, the south of England on the A3, to the West end via St Georges rd, and to the City of London via London rd and Newington causeway at the northern junction. Newington Butts and Walworth Road adjoin the southern junction. The whole junction forms part of the London inner ring rd and part of the boundary of the London congestion charge zone.

The Elephant has two linked London underground stations, on the Northern and Bakerloo lines, and a National rail station served by Southeastern (Kentish Town to Sevenoaks via Catford) and Thameslink (suburban loop to Sutton and Wimbledon), and other Thameslink services to Kent.

Local buildings include Skipton house, part of the Department of Health: Perronet house, an award-winning residential block owned by Southwark Council; a large part of the London South Bank University campus; the London College of communications; the Ministry of sound nightclub; and the Metropolitan Tabernacle. The Cuming museum is nearby on Walworth Road.

The name "Elephant and Castle" is derived from a coaching inn.The earliest surviving record of this name in relation to this area appears in the Court leet Book of the Manor of Walworth, which met at "Elephant and Castle, Newington" on 21 March 1765. The inn's name is sometimes explained as an English corruption of "La Infantana de Castilla", a reference to a Spanish princess with an English connection, such as Eleanor of Castille or Katherine of Aaragon (who before her marriage was *la ynfante doña Catalina de Castille y Aragon*, "*infanta* of Castile and Aragon"), or perhaps the 17th century Maria Anna of Spain. unsuccessfully pursued as a bride by Charles 1. This is considered an improbable etymology. Previously the site was occupied by a blacksmith and cutler – the crest of the Worshipful company of Cutlers features an elephant with a castle (representing a howdah) on its back, which in turn was used because of the use of elephant ivory in handles; this association with the Worshipful Company of Cutlers is considered a far more likely explanation for the name.

[Photo above of the Elephant on the shopping centre's final day]

This was an article that the South London Press ran about me, I was interviewed by their reporter Sam McMasters at their Streatham office. It was all about my building bricks when I worked on the construction of the Heygate estate at the

Elephant/Walworth. I was interviewed by Sam for about half an hour and gave him a general account of my time working there.

This photo/article has pride of place on my front room wall.

- - - - -

Gerry's Cafe

I must give Gerry's working mans cafe a mention, it was situated in Hampton st [Walworth rd end] I used it on and off for about a year way back in 1970. He was a Belfast man and when you walked up to the counter to order your meal [say stewed steak and two veg] his assistant would give you your cuppa tea as you paid for your meal. Then as you turned around to walk over to your table with your cuppa in your hand, Gerry would be pushing by you with your meal in his hand saying right where are you sitting. Talk about "fast food delivery" it was phenomenal .

Gerry retired and went down to either Cornwall or Devon I wanted to keep his memory alive. I think his cafe later became a chippy then a Chinese take away shop.

- - - - -

226

Summing Up

Well folks that is my book over and I hope you have enjoyed my lifetime and adventures of a Gorbals bricklayer in South London [Elephant&Castle/Walwoth etc] I sometimes think of all that I have put into my life I shouldn't be 72 years old but double that, see I'm actually 144 years old.Lol.

Can it really be 52 years ago [as I write] that I landed at Euston railway station a fresh faced young 20 year old bricklayer with my tool bag, level and wondering how is my life going to turn out, well I think overall my life turned out not bad. Sure I made a few mistakes along the way but then again I'm only human but I could never have been sitting behind a desk or working in a bank or factory [nothing wrong with those jobs at all] that wasn't for Danny Gill. See ever since I was a schoolkid sitting in my classroom in Glasgow I had this terrible urge to roam and travel. Some call it "itchy feet syndrome" to me it was "wanderlust" and now I'm in my Autumn years and looking back I think I have fulfilled my wish.

I always had a great belief in myself and having a good trade behind my I found myself travelling to not only other towns and city's but also to other countries to live and work and I'm being quiet honest with you all when I say that I'm really glad that I chose Walworth as my "adopted home" of all the parts of London that I have lived and worked in to me Walworth was/is the best. Of course I'm not being disrespectful to others who live in other parts of London no, not at all but I must say it as I feel. I always got on great with my Cockney boys/girls mates but especially in Walworth.

I remember my first sighting of the Elephant when I worked on the construction of Perronet house and then my first visit to Walworth and East street market and from that first moment I knew I was going to love the place. East st or the Lane as its commonly known was a meeting place to see all my pals, especially in the pubs and all the other Glaswegians I met there. All the times I drank in the Bell, Good Intent, Masons etc and all the laughs I had when the beer was flowing.

Then all the different building sites I worked on and making good money on the way, I'll never forget working on the building of the Heygate, Aylesbury and Salisbury estates and many more, and the brickwork sub contractors I worked with and Dave Sullivan, Tony Carr and Bill Little being the best ones. Of course I also remember the few bad ones I worked with who "knocked" me for my wages but thank God they were few in number.

Then the ladies in my life in South London, Maggie Fitz and a few others [Schhh] before I met my wife Mo and then having our three beautiful daughters Tracy, Susan and Danielle and all my grand children who I love dearly. Flying over from Dublin where I was working to give my Tracy away at her wedding in June 1998, giving my Susan away at her wedding in September 2004. My Danielle not married yet but her and her partner Mitch have two boys so maybe one day I will give her away.?

Then flying over to Australia, working in the scorching heat [which made me enjoy the ice cold beer better]. then having the misfortune to meet up with "Terrible Trudy" who tried to murder me while I was sleeping. The two car crashes I was in when living in Oz but lived to tell the tale. Then making the mistake of moving back in with Maggie Fitz when I came back.

My two trips over to Germany all the schnapps and beer I drank when living there, getting "knocked for our wages" with the Dutchman, learning to speak German and the kindness shown to me by the German people. Getting "mugged" for my money in the German bar when I was trying to kiss the "house girl" who called me "Kleine Elvis".

Losing my house keys when living at Mrs Ullmans digs and being told you have a weeks notice to leave my digs.

Then moving into "The Whitehouse" and all the shenanigans that happened in there but also liking living there with an evening meal every night and the Albert arms round the corner.

Then moving back onto the Heygate estate again and meeting up with all my old neighbours and drinking in the Butts with my old bricklaying pal Tommy Marks.Then drinking back down Walworth rd in the Kings head, the Rock/Liam Og's, in the Red Lion and all my Irish mates.

Moving over to Ireland to live and work and coming back to lose my flat on the Heygate and living out at Penge with my own cleaning lady.

Moving into the Lord Nelson pub on the Old Kent rd and Pat the lovely landlady, then moving over to East London to live and work but coming back to live in East st when Andy Storrie told me big Davy Sherry was in jail and his flat needed looking after.

Then moving into the 5 Bells pub at New cross and living there but the arthritis in my knees playing me up bad and that terrible recession which saw an end to my working career.

Then finally moving into sheltered housing out at Lee green [Lewisham] where I have a beautiful little self-contained flat.

[Photo of my self contained flat or my Palace as I call it]

So folks that was some of the memories that have always stayed in my mind during my lifetime and adventures, but do you know the funny thing was that every time I came back from another country or other part of London where I had been working I always made a bee-line back to South London as that was my "adopted home".

Of course as I said previously when my time comes my three daughters will take my ashes back to the Gorbals and be scattered outside of St Francis Church as that is where my Ma and Da were married and I was baptized.

Many thanks to you all for taking the time to read my lifetime and adventures it sure has been a ball and I'm extremely happy to have enjoyed such a great life. Just remember whatever the years may change our memories are forever.

Danny Gill
2020
God bless all. x

- - - - -

Printed in Great Britain
by Amazon